D1314812

Manager's Official Guide to Team Working

MANAGER'S
OFFICIAL GUIDE
TO
TEAM WORKING

JERRY SPIEGEL, PH.D.
&
CRESENCIO TORRES, PH.D.

Johannesburg • Oxford
San Diego • Sydney • Toronto

Copyright © 1994 by Pfeiffer & Company

ISBN 0-88390-408-X

Library of Congress Catalog Card Number 93-087074

Printed in the United States of America

Pfeiffer & Company
International Publishers
8517 Production Avenue
San Diego, California 92121-2280
USA
(619) 578-5900; FAX (619) 578-2042

This book is printed on acid-free, recycled stock that meets or
exceeds the minimum GPO and EPA specification for recycled paper.

TABLE OF CONTENTS

PREFACE

Organization leaders are realizing that employees at all levels must be contributing and participating members of the work force if their organizations are to be competitive in the world marketplace. In addition, leaders are also becoming aware that teams offer many advantages over more traditional ways of organizing labor: skills and tasks are widely distributed among all team members; team members are held accountable for maintaining and improving the processes for which they are responsible; and team members share leadership and management responsibilities, which will reduce the number of supervisory personnel.

From an ideal perspective, effective teams are cohesive, efficient, and productive. A team's output can be measured in terms of both quality and quantity. Teams comprise individuals who are both competent and knowledgeable in their duties. Furthermore, the quality of team decision making is high, and team members share in the knowledge that the work they do together is superior.

As managers will verify, team-development efforts work. Team development helps members to build on their strengths. It encourages them to strengthen their weaknesses and manage their problems together. An important outcome is that team development and teamwork promote a better understanding between individuals—the most critical factor in the success of any organization.

Although all teams follow a logical development process, it is important for managers and team leaders to recognize that each team will have a unique set of circumstance that will effect its individual developmental process.

Team development is the single most powerful tool that can bring a team together in the pursuit of common goals. This book will provide you with ideas and methods for increasing the effectiveness of your team-development efforts.

INTRODUCTION

This book is written for managers, supervisors, and team leaders who find themselves responsible for developing effective work groups or teams. It provides important information for implementing the team-development process.

In chapter one, we define the term "team" as differentiated from other groups in the workplace, examine the characteristics of effective teams, tell when to form a team, describe how to form a team that works, examine the key areas of organizational resistance, discuss the benefits of teams to the organization, and discuss the benefits of teams for individuals.

In chapter two, we define team formation and assessment, examine team-recruitment considerations, review team-selection criteria, discuss the importance of assessment, tell when to assess and how to do it, and examine the form and function of different organizational designs based on a sports analogy.

In chapter three, we define effective communication and present a six-step communication model that includes a discussion of barriers to effective communication and methods for overcoming them.

In chapter four, we define team development, describe the stages of team development, and discuss what leaders can do to facilitate the stages.

In chapter five, we define team-member roles, describe the differences between task and process, specify seven task roles, describe four positive process roles, describe five negative process roles, and present methods for managing negative process behaviors.

In chapter six, we define decision making, describe an eight-step decision-making model, discuss five decision-making procedures, examine four advantages of participatory decision making, and tell how to implement decisions.

In chapter seven, we define conflict, describe three views of conflict, examine six causes of conflict, identify five conflict strategies, discuss when to use the strategies, and describe a six-step process for managing team conflict.

In chapter eight, we define the term "team meeting," describe the purpose of team meetings, tell how to plan meetings, discuss how to select the right people to attend, emphasize the need for an agenda, and discuss meeting management.

In chapter nine, we define problem solving, examine a seven-step process that can be used by team members in any problem-solving situation, and discuss how to make the process work.

In our concluding chapter, chapter ten, we define the term "politics of participation," examine eleven critical factors that are essential when considering a team-structured organization, and describe four critical roles that individuals play in facilitating the change process.

At the end of each chapter, we have included a "Quick Review" section for easy reference. These offer brief synopses of the chapters for the convenience of those readers who have limited time.

1

TEAMS AND TEAMWORK

Organizations that exist in competitive markets demand a high level of performance from their employees. Simply complying with rules and obeying supervisors is no longer enough; organizations need employees who are highly committed and willing to work in new ways. The effective use of "teams" in the workplace will greatly increase the probability that organizations will achieve their strategic goals.

Chapter 1 does the following:

- Defines the term "team" as differentiated from other groups in the workplace;
- Examines the characteristics of effective teams;
- Tells when to form a team;
- Describes how to form a team that works;
- Examines the primary areas of resistance in the organization;
- Discusses the benefits of teams to the organization; and
- Discusses the benefits of teams for individuals.

DEFINITION OF A TEAM

It is important to accurately define what we mean by the word "team" and how teams differ from other groups in the workplace. A "group" is a number of individuals who are together because of common characteristics or interests. A "team" is a specific type of work group; it must be organized and managed differently from other types of work groups.

Many people in organizations use the word "teams" to describe groups in which they participate. Some of these groups can be described more accurately by the functions they perform, such as "the picnic committee" or "the marketing group."

To better understand the differences between teams and other work groups, we need to examine the characteristics of teams and the characteristics of various work groups such as committees, task forces, process-improvement groups, and department-improvement groups.

Committees

The most common work group is the committee. Committees are organized by management for specific purposes and have scheduled meetings. They are made up of individuals who are selected by management to investigate, advise, and report their findings. Committees can be ad hoc (short-term) or ongoing (long-term).

Task Forces

A task force is a group formed by upper management to resolve a major problem immediately. Employees are temporarily excused from their regular assignments to work as task-force members. The task force is solely responsible for developing a long-term plan to solve the problem. Often, the task force also is responsible for implementing the solution.

Process-Improvement Groups

A process-improvement group is made up of experienced people from different departments or functions. The chairperson and members are appointed by management to improve quality, decrease waste, and improve productivity in processes that affect all the departments or functions.

Department-Improvement Groups

A department-improvement group is made up of the members of a department. The group identifies problems that decrease departmental productivity both within the department and with customers. The department's manager is responsible for forming the group, and department members may be required to participate in the group's activities.

Teams

A work team is a group of individuals who work together, who have the same work *objectives*, and whose work is *mutually dependent.* The team members are joined in a coordinated effort, much like a team in a contest or competition. In the workplace, the contest is not against other teams within the organization but against waste, poor quality, delays, the need to redo work, low productivity, and the competitors in the marketplace.

A team is the most advanced form of group.

CHARACTERISTICS OF EFFECTIVE TEAMS

Some of the characteristics of effective teams are given on the following page.

Team members share a common identity. Team members identify themselves as belonging to the team.

Team members have common goals and objectives. Effective teams have clearly defined directions and measurable outcomes.

Team members share common leadership. Effective team leaders facilitate and support team efforts.

Team members share successes and failures. Team members are held jointly responsible for the achievement of their objectives.

Team members cooperate and collaborate. Teams must perform complex tasks that require high degrees of interdependence and cooperation among team members.

Teams have membership roles. Effective team members know their roles and how they relate to the task.

Teams make decisions effectively. Effective teams use decision-making processes that facilitate task accomplishment.

Teams are made of diverse people. Effective teams are made up of individuals who have different backgrounds and work experiences.

WHEN TO FORM A TEAM

A team should be formed only when a group of individuals have to work together in a coordinated effort to achieve specified outcomes. A team does not need to be formed if the individuals can work separately or if they can do the work equally as well in some other form of group. Forming a team for the sake of forming a team is likely to result in disgruntled and frustrated members because there is no "real" reason for the team to exist.

A team will have a greater chance to succeed if the following conditions are present:

- A specified, measurable objective that can be best achieved by a team effort;
- An organizational culture that supports the team concept;
- Sufficient time for adequate training, debating, and discussion; and
- Knowledge and use of various problem-solving techniques.

FORMING A TEAM THAT WORKS

Even if an organization meets all of the previously discussed conditions for developing a team, a number of other issues must be considered.

An effective team operates in an atmosphere of mutual respect; members identify with one another and with the team as a whole. In addition, the team members develop a process for working together and interdependently recognize and use one anothers' knowledge and skills to achieve their designated objectives. The following are four traits that characterize effective teams:

- Commitment to the team,
- Decisions made by consensus,

- A process for managing conflict and creativity, and

- Effective discussion procedures.

Commitment to the team. Commitment to the team generates feelings of empowerment for the team members. Commitment comes from being recognized as a valued member who contributes to task accomplishment.

Decisions made by consensus. When a decision is made by consensus, team members resolve their conflicts by reaching mutual consent. Consensus allows team members to openly share opinions and resolve issues with the outcome of satisfying all members.

A process for managing conflict and creativity. Every team will encounter conflict during its existence. Conflict is healthy when matched with the willingness to resolve problems. Creativity is generated by the tension created by dissonance within the team.

Effective discussion procedures. Effective discussions within the team facilitate commitment, consensus, conflict resolution, and creativity. Teamwork cannot be achieved if individual members are unable to talk to one another in an appropriate and responsible manner.

KEY AREAS OF RESISTANCE IN ORGANIZATIONS

It is important to realize that not all organizational forces will be in favor of developing the team concept or making systems changes. Resistance to the formation and use of teams can come from three significant areas: organizational structure, management and supervision, and individual workers.

Organizational Structure

Conditions that mitigate against the team concept include:

- Hierarchical and bureaucratic structures,
- Top-down management practices,
- A nonflexible, no-risk corporate culture,
- One-way communication—usually down, and
- Departmental isolation.

Management and Supervision

Managers and supervisors can sabotage team efforts because of:

- Fear of losing power and status,
- Fear that they will no longer be needed,
- Failure to delegate authority and responsibility,
- Failure to provide adequate training and support,
- Failure to hold the team accountable, and
- Failure to communicate corporate goals clearly and to set objectives adequately.

Individual Workers

Employees may resist the team concept because they:

- Fear losing individual rewards and recognition,

- Fear losing individuality,
- Fear that teams will create more work,
- Fear assuming responsibility, and
- Fear conflict.

BENEFITS OF TEAMS TO THE ORGANIZATION

Organizations that use teams can expect gains in efficiency and, therefore, a positive impact on the organizational bottom line. Benefits can take the form of increased productivity, improved service and product quality, increased employee morale, or reduced overhead.

Increased Productivity

Increased productivity can be defined as the ability to furnish results, benefits, or profits in abundance. Teams can increase their productivity by improving work methods and procedures, which in turn allows them to improve efficiency, rate of output, and product and service quality, thereby cutting waste and reducing the need to redo tasks.

Increased Quality

High and consistent quality can be defined as the degree to which a product or service meets the customer's requirements and specifications. Effective teams can increase the quality of products and services because their members are able to implement quality-control improvements.

Teams also can increase quality because their members have greater authority and control over the work processes, thereby increasing individual accountability for production quality. Team members can identify with and feel pride in the production of a product or service with which they are involved.

Increased Employee Morale

Employee morale can be defined as the positive emotional condition of a person or a group with regard to that person's or group's tasks on the job. Effective teams can help to create satisfying and rewarding work environments, thereby producing positive employee attitudes, increasing productivity, and reducing costs.

Membership in teams helps to satisfy individual needs to belong, to interact with others, to receive recognition, and to achieve. Praise from team members also can be a strong source of motivation; conversely, team members know that they can be replaced for poor performance. Finally, because the use of teams produces more satisfied employees, the result is less employee turnover.

Reduced Overhead

Overhead can be defined as any business expense that is not chargeable to a particular sector of the production process. Obviously, reduction of overhead results in an increased bottom line.

In organizations that use teams, many of the tasks that are traditionally assigned to the supervisory staff can be assigned directly to the teams themselves, thereby effecting a significant reduction in overhead. Significant gains can be achieved by reducing support staff and supervisory personnel.

BENEFITS OF TEAMS TO INDIVIDUALS

The use of teams in organizations can impact everyone involved. Specifically, individuals benefit as follows:

- Work is less stressful.
- Responsibility is shared.
- Team members have greater feelings of self-worth.
- Rewards and recognition are shared.
- Team members have the ability to influence one another.
- All of the team members experience a sense of accomplishment.

Although there is no one path to achieving high production, high quality, reduced overhead, and high morale, the use of teams has proven to contribute to all these outcomes in organizations.

QUICK REVIEW

Definition of a Team

A team is a specific form of work group that must be organized and managed differently from other types of work groups. It is made up of individuals who work together in a coordinated effort — who constitute one side in a type of contest. The contest is not against other teams within the organization but against waste, poor quality, delays, the need to redo work, low productivity, and with competitors in the market-place.

Characteristics of Effective Teams

Some characteristics of effective teams are as follows:

- Team members share a common identity.
- Team members have common goals and objectives.
- Team members share common leadership.
- Team members share successes and failures.
- Team members cooperate and collaborate.
- Teams have membership roles.
- Teams make decisions effectively.
- Teams are made of diverse people.

When To Form a Team

Teams will have greater chance to succeed if the conditions given on the following page are present.

- A specified, measurable objective that can be best achieved by a team effort;
- An organizational culture that supports the team concept;
- Sufficient time for adequate training, debating, and discussion; and
- Knowledge and use of problem-solving techniques.

Forming a Team That Works

Four traits characterize effective teams; they are as follows:

- Commitment to the team,
- Decisions made by consensus,
- A process for managing conflict and creativity, and
- Effective discussion procedures.

Key Areas of Resistance in Organizations

The three key areas of resistance in organizations are as follows:

- Organizational structure,
- Management and supervision, and
- Individual workers.

Benefits of Teams to the Organization

The benefits to the organization are as follows:

- Increased productivity,
- Increased quality,

- Increased employee morale, and
- Reduced overhead.

Benefits of Teams to Individuals

The benefits to the individual are as follows:

- Work is less stressful.
- Responsibility is shared.
- Team members have greater feelings of self-worth.
- Rewards and recognition are shared.
- Team members have the ability to influence one another.
- All of the team members experience a sense of accomplishment.

2

TEAM FORMATION
AND
ASSESSMENT

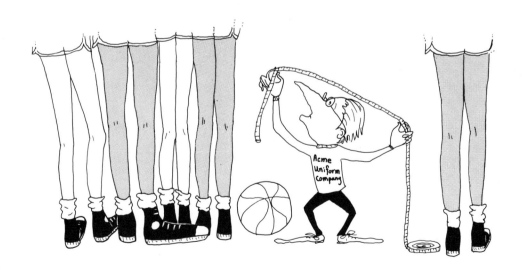

Once the decision to use teams has been made, the manager or the team leader has to select and assess potential team members and determine the appropriate work design model for the team.

Chapter 2 does the following:

- Defines team formation and assessment;
- Examines team recruitment considerations;
- Reviews team selection criteria;
- Discusses the importance of assessment;
- Tells when and how to assess teams; and
- Presents a model of form and function to determine different organizational team designs based on a sports analogy.

DEFINITION OF TEAM FORMATION AND ASSESSMENT

Team formation is the process by which individuals are recruited, selected, and evaluated as potential team members. Assessment is the method used to determine the readiness level of selected team members to perform their work.

TEAM RECRUITMENT CONSIDERATIONS

When forming a team, the manager or team leader must consider the following two items:

- The level of technical ability of potential team members, and
- The level of interpersonal skills of the potential team members.

Because the levels of technical expertise and inter-personal skills of team members will dictate the amount of direction and training that must be provided, the manager or team leader will need to select individuals who have a moderate to high degree of both kinds of skills or a moderate to high degree of willingness to learn.

It is not always possible to select fully trained team members, so the manager or team leader must consider how much time and what kind of resources he or she must provide to them. Because the nature of technical skills required to effectively perform work tasks varies from organization to organization, it is the manager's or the team leader's responsibility to decide what constitutes expertise. Team members can be recruited in two ways: through job postings or by individual invitation.

Many organizations post job openings whenever a position is available. The advantages of job posting are as follows:

- Everyone has an opportunity to apply.
- A climate of trust is created.
- The process may uncover unrecognized talent.
- All potential members would be volunteers.

The disadvantages of job posting are as follows:

- There may be too little or too great a response.
- A time-consuming selection process may occur if too many people respond.
- The manager or team leader may have to reject some volunteers.

Another way to recruit team members is to send each prospective individual an invitation. The advantages of individual invitations are as follows:

- Individuals with the most appropriate technical and human interaction skills are selected.
- The selection process is time efficient.
- Individuals who already buy into the team concept can be selected.
- Individuals have a choice to be on the team or not to be on the team.

The disadvantages of individual invitation are as follows:

- It perpetuates a climate of secrecy.
- Qualified individuals may not be discovered.
- A request to join the team may be perceived as preferential treatment by individuals who were not asked to join the team.

TEAM SELECTION CRITERIA

When selecting team members, the manager or team leader will need to consider some specific criteria that facilitate team interaction and teamwork. Four criteria to consider when selecting potential team members are as follows: personal attributes, interpersonal behaviors, communication skills, and administrative skills.

Personal Attributes

Standards: What are the individual's values in terms of working with others on a team?

Initiative: Is the individual proactive or reactive when problem solving?

Organizational Identification: Is the individual committed to achieving the organization's goals?

Tolerance for Stress: Does the individual have methods for managing the stress that will be created by adopting the team concept?

Interpersonal Behaviors

Influence: What methods does the individual use to influence others?

Sensitivity: Does the individual display sensitivity to others' feelings and ideas?

Developing Others: Has the individual served as a mentor or coach to subordinates or peers?

Trustworthiness: Does the individual fulfill his or her commitments?

Communication Skills

Dialogue Skills: Does the individual have the ability or potential to communicate effectively in both formal and informal work settings?

Presentation Skills: Can the individual present ideas and concepts to others in a clear and focused manner?

Writing Skills: How effective is the individual when putting thoughts and ideas in written form?

Reading Skills: How effective is the individual in acquiring new knowledge through reading?

Administrative Skills

Planning: Does the individual have skills in developing strategies for reaching designated outcomes?

Organizing: How skilled is the individual in aligning resources with a plan?

Implementing: Does the individual have an "action orientation"?

Delegating: Does the individual have the ability to assign appropriate tasks to himself or herself and others?

AUTHORS' NOTE

The selection of willing and able team members is important to the overall level of success of the team and the team effort. In order to develop an effective and efficient team, the manager or team leader must choose individuals with skills in the four areas previously mentioned or those who are willing and able to be trained. Failure to pay attention in the beginning will serve only to subvert the team effort in the end.

Evaluating: Does the individual have the ability to learn from successes and failures?

THE IMPORTANCE OF ASSESSMENT

Assessment is an important process because it provides the manager or the team leader with a basic understanding of what type of team or group to form, and the readiness level of the team to perform its functions and meet its objectives.

Based on assessment results, the manager or the team leader can measure the gap between the ideal expectation of how individuals "should be" organized and the present reality of how they operate. Adequate up-front assessment provides information to the manager or team leader about how to narrow this gap.

For example, if a manager determines that forming a team is required, he or she can first assess the readiness level of all the individuals involved in performing the job tasks required of the team. If the readiness level is low, the manager can provide training and coaching to close the gap between the present skill levels and the desired skill levels of the team members. Similarly, if those individuals who will be working together are assessed as having poor meeting-management skills, for example, future training could be targeted at developing those skills.

WHEN AND HOW TO ASSESS TEAMS

The logical place to start identifying what type of group is needed begins with the question, "What is the purpose for organizing a group or team?" The answer to this question will help to determine whether or not to form a team or form another type of work group. The manager or team leader should use the following guidelines when deciding on the purpose for organizing a group or team and what type of work group or team to form:

- To investigate, advise, and report findings to management, form a *committee;*

- To solve major problems immediately, form a *task force;*

- To qualify the process, improve quality, decrease waste, or improve productivity across departmental lines, form a *process-improvement group;*

- To provide a focus and a means for employees to contribute to an ongoing activity directed at increasing the quality and productivity of the department, form a *department-improvement group;*

- To organize diverse people with various knowledge and skills who must meet business objectives that require a focused approach, consider using *teams.*

Another level of assessment that focuses on individuals can best be accomplished by considering the following four categories: (1) the technical ability of individuals to accomplish the work, (2) the ability of individuals to integrate work with others toward a common outcome, (3) the ability of individuals to manage people, and (4) the congruity between the form the team takes and the function it performs. Remember, in determining the type of work-team configuration that is most appropriate for organizing personnel, form should always follow function.

Technical Ability

Technical ability means the level of skill demonstrated by each individual when accomplishing his or her work. This level of expertise will dictate the amount of direction or training that will be required to meet the team's goals. If individuals are assessed as not skilled enough to perform their jobs, they will need both formal training as well as on-the-job direction. To be successful, the manager or team leader will need to train, coach, and closely monitor the efforts of the individuals in training.

On the other hand, if individuals are assessed as having high skill levels in their areas of expertise, the manager or team leader will need to provide less remedial support and more delegating and coaching.

AUTHORS' NOTE

As a rule, the more skilled the team members are in doing their work, the more autonomy they should be given to accomplish their work. All too often managers practice micro-management techniques that interfere with individuals and their work.

Ability To Integrate Work

This area of assessment has to do with how aware and knowledgeable managers or team leaders are of potential team members' expertise, knowledge base, and skill levels. Assessment in this area requires a close look at each individual and what he or she can contribute to the overall team effort.

Shared knowledge and experience will improve the integration of ideas and concepts, which will lead to greater team synergy and success. Managers or team leaders must ensure that opportunities for information exchange among team members occur.

Ability To Manage People

Managing people means the ability to orchestrate a team's meetings, communication processes, problem solving, decision making, conflict resolution, and other aspects of team involvement.

These issues are common to all work groups and teams and must be managed or, in spite of a high degree of technical expertise among team members, the team will not succeed.

If an ongoing team is assessed as having a low level of interpersonal experience and skills, it will require both a high degree of conceptual knowledge as well as skill training if the team is to be successful.

For example, if a team has experience in meeting-management skills, the function of the manager or team leader can be rotated. On the other hand, if the team members are inexperienced and unskilled in this area, the manager or team leader must operate from a more central position in the team. In this case, the addition of a trained facilitator would greatly increase the team's chances for meeting its desired outcomes.

AUTHORS' NOTE

Another rule is that the more skilled a team is in managing its own interpersonal dynamics, the more self-managing the team can become. The less able the team is in managing the interpersonal dynamics, the more central and active the leadership must be.

FORM AND FUNCTION—A SPORTS ANALOGY

Organizations often function without an awareness of the basic work-design models under which they can choose to operate. They could function more effectively if they were aware of the choices available to them. As previously mentioned, the form that a team takes should follow the function that the team is expected to carry out. The use of athletic team models can illustrate the strengths and weaknesses of different work designs.

Baseball

The individual is the basic unit in a baseball team. Player interaction is minimal, and usually only two or three players on the same team are involved in any one play. Team success (scoring) is determined by totaling each team's performance (runs scored), and team coordination is produced by the design of the play itself.

In examining the roles of baseball-team members, one notices that not all players can play every position. The pitcher and catcher, for example, are trained in highly specialized positions, whereas other team members may be rotated in and out of various positions. Outfielders may prefer a specific field but they are capable of playing any outfield position. Infielders, on the other hand, have more specialized roles and are less apt to change positions. However, infielders support one another when the ball is in play such as in a swiftly executed double play.

Effective baseball-type work teams have a number of common characteristics:

Autonomy: Each of the team members works relatively independently.

Initiative: Team members are expected to exercise their knowledge and influence in their areas of expertise.

Flexibility: Members must be able to carry out a variety of independent tasks, the order and priorities of which can change unpredictably.

Contribution: All tasks performed by team members culminate in an end product.

Infrequent Interaction: Interactions between members are brief and infrequent. However, team members are aware of others' actions.

The key to success with the baseball-team model is the effective management of task interdependence—the process of integrating the parts to compose a whole. This type of work team relies on pooled independence. In this model, the parts are relatively independent of one another but make contributions to the overall effort. Pooled independence implies that the individuals are soloists who, if they were musicians, would be like those who work together in a rock and roll band.

Football

Although actions by individuals are important in football, this game demands greater team interaction than does baseball. In the game of football, every player on the field participates actively in every play. Success (scoring) is determined by the team's ability to perform as a single unit. A good football team consists of a defense that acts as a wall through which the opposing team cannot penetrate and an aggressive offense that finds the other team's weak spots and takes advantage of them. Team coordination is achieved under the planning and direction of coaches and specialists who also must function as a unified force to communicate their messages.

Work teams based on the football-team model consist of individuals who occupy distinct positions; the ordering and hierarchy of these positions are determined by the skills needed to accomplish the team's task. Key positions on the team are awarded to individuals who have mastered specialized technical skills. These key players are supported by individuals whose jobs are less technically complex and more interchangeable.

On a football team the quarterback holds the most important position. The quarterback determines each play's strategy, calls signals, and handles the ball on every play. The group of players that is next highest in importance (backfield runners, pass receivers, and blockers) has varying levels of significance; a player may be critical in one play and less so on another. Although the contribution of the left tackle or guard is always critical to the success of the play, that player never carries the ball.

Effective football-type work teams have a number of common characteristics:

Effective Planning: Execution of individual tasks is coordinated through a comprehensive, prerehearsed plan of action.

Efficient Coordination of Complex Parts: Success can be achieved only if all team members' actions are carefully coordinated.

Predetermined Sequence of Action: Tasks must be carried out in a controlled order.

Equal Contribution Among Team Members: All team members must pull their own weight.

Constant Communication: Team members must interact frequently and must communicate appropriately to suit the task at hand.

The key to success when implementing the football-team model is the effective management of specialized tasks. A group patterned after a football team stresses controlled and sequential interdependence. Each team member relies heavily on the cooperation of others in order to complete tasks successfully.

QUICK REVIEW

Definition of Team Formation and Assessment

Team formation is the process by which individuals are recruited, selected, and evaluated as potential team members. Assessment is the method used to determine the readiness level of selected team members to perform their work.

Team Recruitment Considerations

When forming a team, the manager or team leader must consider the following two items:

- The level of technical ability of potential team members, and
- The level of interpersonal skills of potential team members.

Team Selection Criteria

When selecting team members, the manager or team leader should consider the following four criteria:

- Personal attributes,
- Interpersonal behaviors,
- Communication skills, and
- Administrative skills.

The Importance of Assessment

Assessment is important because it provides managers and team leaders with a basic understanding of how to:

- Determine what type of team or group to form, and
- Assess the readiness level of the team to perform its function and meet its objective.

When and How To Assess Teams

The manager or team leader should use the following guidelines when deciding what type of work group or team to form:

- If the group's purpose is to investigate, advise, and report findings to management, form a *committee.*
- If the group's purpose is to solve major problems immediately, form a *task force.*
- If the group's purpose is to qualify the process, improve quality, decrease waste, or improve productivity across departmental lines, form a *process-improvement group.*
- If the group's purpose is to provide a focus and a means for employees to contribute to an ongoing activity directed at increasing the quality and productivity of the department, form a *department-improvement group.*
- If the group's purpose is to organize diverse people with various knowledge and skills who must meet business objectives that require a focused approach, consider using *teams.*

In addition, it is important to focus on a second-level assessment and to consider the following:

- The technical ability of individuals to accomplish the work;
- The ability of individuals to integrate work with others toward common outcomes;

- The ability of individuals to manage people; and
- The congruity between the form the team takes and the function it performs.

Form should always follow function.

Form and Function—A Sports Analogy

The use of athletic team models can illustrate the strengths and weaknesses of different work designs. Each sports team model shares a number of common characteristics:

Baseball

Autonomy: Each of the team members works relatively independently.

Initiative: Team members are expected to exercise their knowledge and influence in their area of expertise.

Flexibility: Team members must be able to carry out a variety of independent tasks, the order and priorities of which can change unpredictably.

Contribution: All tasks performed by team members culminate in an end product.

Infrequent Interaction: Interactions between members are brief and infrequent. However, team members are aware of others' actions.

Football

Effective Planning: Execution of individual tasks is coordinated through a comprehensive, prerehearsed plan of action.

Efficient Coordination of Complex Parts: Success can be achieved only if all members' actions are carefully coordinated.

Predetermined Sequence of Action: Tasks must be carried out in a controlled order.

Equal Contribution Among Members: All team members must pull their own weight.

Constant Communication: Members must interact frequently and must communicate appropriately to suit the task at hand.

3

EFFECTIVE TEAM COMMUNICATION

Once a team has been formed and assessed, its pursuit of excellence depends on the quality and flow of its communication processes. Team members must continually exchange ideas, opinions, and feelings about the work of the team. To a large extent, the quality and quantity of the team's output depends on the quality of information team members share. Effective communication is essential for decision making and other aspects of team development.

Chapter 3 does the following:

- Defines effective communication; and

- Reviews a six-step communication model.

DEFINITION OF EFFECTIVE COMMUNICATION

Effective communication is the verbal and nonverbal exchange of information between two or more people that is satisfactorily received and acted on by all parties. Communication includes the transference and understanding of meaning between the giver of the communication and the receiver of it. An idea, no matter how good, is useless until it is understood by others.

THE SIX-STEP COMMUNICATION MODEL

In order to better explain the dynamics of the communication process, a six-step communication model that describes how people share information is given on the following page. In addition, some barriers to effective communication and the methods for overcoming them are discussed.

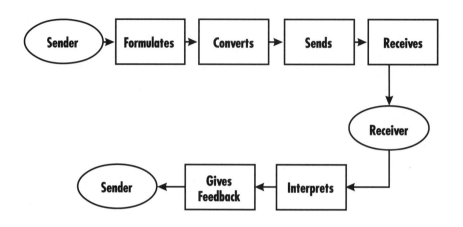

Six-Step Communication Model

Step 1: Formulating the Information

The sender formulates an idea, opinion, fact, or feeling.

Step 2: Converting the Information

The sender converts the information into symbolic verbal or nonverbal language.

Step 3: Sending the Information

The sender transmits the message.

Step 4: Receiving the Information

The other person receives the symbolic verbal or nonverbal message.

Step 5: Interpreting and Understanding the Information

The receiver interprets the message and either understands it or does not understand it.

Step 6: Sending Feedback

The receiver sends a message back to the sender to check the sender's understanding.

A closer examination of each step will clarify what factors contribute to effective communication.

Step 1: Formulating the Information

In this step, the sender thinks about what he or she wants to say. He or she needs to consider three factors before deciding to communicate the information: content, clarity, and timing.

Content: Content refers to the subject of the information that is to be communicated. In the context of working within a team, the sender should always evaluate the importance of the information and how it might help the team to achieve its goals. If the content is valid and contributes to a better understanding of the goals, it should be communicated to the team.

Clarity: Clarity refers to the sender's ability to share information clearly with others. If a person is not clear about the message that he or she will share, others will have a difficult time understanding it. It is important for the sender to think the idea through fully before attempting to share it with others. When ideas that are not clear are shared, it is important that the sender let others know that the information is incomplete or unclear.

Timing: Timing refers to the appropriateness of the information being shared as it relates to the subject under discussion. Some ideas may be excellent but may be shared at the wrong time. Good ideas should be saved and shared when it is appropriate.

Step 2: Converting the Information

In the second step, the sender converts information into symbolic verbal or nonverbal language. Symbolic language is the code or group of symbols that the sender uses to transfer the content and meaning of his or her message. For example, when we write a message, the written letter is the symbol used. When we speak and gesture, our voice and our body language are the symbols used to transfer meaning.

The three symbolic categories in the communication process that we will discuss are body language, vocal expression, and words or language.

Body Language: Almost 80 percent of communication is derived from the body language of the sender. Body language includes posture, facial expressions, gestures, use of space, eye contact, and other body movements. It is said that people can lie with words but not with the language conveyed by their bodies. An astute observer of people often can diagnose the emotional states of others merely by observing nonverbal cues.

Nonverbal behaviors that demonstrate receptivity to effective communication include appropriate eye contact, slight gesturing of the head when listening to someone, appropriate facial expressions, and facing the person with an open posture.

Nonverbal behaviors that block effective communication include lack of eye contact; a negative shaking of the head; facial expressions that convey arrogance, disapproval, or anger; and turning away from the speaker while maintaining a closed posture.

Vocal Expression: The spoken word in the communication process represents about 20 percent of the message. Vocal expression includes the volume, pitch, tone, and tempo of the voice and frequency of pauses.

Vocal expression often has greater impact on the receiver than the content of the spoken words. Consider the team member who asks a question and receives a reply such as "What do you mean by that?" Such a reply can be interpreted to mean anything from defensiveness to inquiry, depending on the vocal expression.

Vocal expressions that demonstrate receptivity to more open communication are as follows:

AUTHORS' NOTE

All of the above behaviors, including how people space themselves in terms of physical distance, have meaning, but what is considered proper must be evaluated in terms of the cultural norms of the people involved. For example, what is a "business-like distance" in some European countries would be viewed as "intimate" in many parts of North America. It is important for people to be aware of the nonverbal aspects of communication in the context of the culture they are in. In addition, it is important to recognize that people from different cultures have various responses to direct eye contact. For example, in North America maintaining eye contact when communicating is highly valued; in some other cultures it is avoided.

- Speaking in a volume that is appropriate to the situation (one that is loud enough to be heard but not overbearing);
- Speaking slowly enough to be understood but fast enough to keep the person's attention;
- Using a pitch and tone of voice that conveys sincerity and understanding rather than anger or sarcasm; and
- Using enough pauses to allow the receiver to paraphrase or ask questions for clarity.

Vocal expressions that block effective communication include speaking in a loud and fast voice; using high or aggressive tones; and using infrequent pauses.

Words or Language: Only a small percent of the meaning of communication is actually derived from the words used by the sender of the message. Nevertheless, words are critical to conveying ideas, information, and opinions.

Fundamentally, it is important for team members to communicate in one common language such as English or Spanish. If team members speak different languages, it is imperative that one language be designated as the official language for the team. It is important that all members be fluent in that designated language. If some team members are not fluent, they continually will be left out of the team's communication process.

Even if all the team members speak the same language, their vocabulary and language sophistication can vary based on their educations, experiences, and regional and ethnic variations. For example, a team made up of English-speaking Americans, Britishers, and Australians would still have communication difficulties based on the team's cultural difference.

Teams that are made up of individuals in the same profession or line of work usually have a common language based on the members' training and backgrounds. This often contributes to more effective communication between individuals. Teams made up of people from diverse backgrounds will often have more difficulty with communication because the members will not understand one anothers' language. Team members need to use simple words that can be understood by all members rather than complex words that may be understood by just a few.

AUTHORS' NOTE

Teams in the workplace are increasingly made up of members from diverse educational, ethnic, and professional backgrounds. The development of a common language is critical to the success of the team. One approach is to offer language classes to all team members who do not speak the chosen language of the team.

Step 3: Sending the Information

Sending information is a skill that can be learned and developed by all team members. To be most effective, however, the sender must ask himself or herself the following questions before the communication begins.

- Is the form of expression being used appropriate for the receiver?

If the answer is no, the sender should determine his or her method of presentation before attempting to convey the message to the receiver. This step is critical if the sender wants the receiver to understand what he or she is trying to say.

- Is too much or too little information being communicated?

If the sender is doing either of these, the receiver will have a harder time understanding what the sender is trying to say. Too little information will cause the receiver to try to fill in the blanks, which may lead to confusion and misunderstanding.

Too much information can cause the receiver to become overloaded, bored, or to dismiss the information. The sender should keep the message simple and to the point.

- Is the receiver paying attention?

If the sender does not have the receiver's attention, his or her message will not be heard. A noisy, distracting, or physically uncomfortable environment will make it more difficult for the receiver to focus on the information being transmitted.

Another consideration is the receiver's state of mind. If he or she is daydreaming or inattentive he or she probably will not hear what the speaker is saying. This can be overcome by politely gaining the attention of the receiver and stating that the information being shared is important.

Step 4: Receiving the Information

Receiving and interpreting information is a skill that can be learned and developed. To be most effective, however, the receiver should ask himself or herself the following questions once the communication has begun.

- Am I paying attention?
- Am I listening in an active or passive manner?

PAYING ATTENTION

Paying attention to what someone says is considered basic to any communication interaction. However, there are a number of factors that will distract the receiver's ability to hear the message that the sender has communicated. The four most significant are as follows: a noisy or distracting environment, daydreaming, simultaneously thinking of a response, and physical or emotional distraction.

A Noisy or Distracting Environment: A noisy environment is a barrier to effective communication. If the surroundings prohibit talking, do not attempt to talk. The sender should delay, postpone, or move the meeting to a place better suited for communication.

Daydreaming: When a receiver finds that he or she is thinking about unrelated ideas during the communication process, it means that he or she probably will not hear or understand what is being communicated. If and when a receiver realizes that he or she is not paying attention, the receiver should refocus his or her attention on the sender and the message being sent. Reengaging techniques include asking questions, taking notes, observing the nonverbal body language of the sender, shifting body position, or taking a break.

Thinking of a Response: A common distraction often experienced by the receiver is thinking about how to respond to the sender while the sender is still talking. It is usually difficult to interpret and respond to a message before it has been completely transmitted. The receiver should allow the sender the opportunity to complete the message before considering a response.

Physical or Emotional Distress: If the receiver is in a state of physical or emotional discomfort, his or her ability to pay attention to anyone's message will be diminished. The receiver should reschedule any meetings if he or she is feeling distracted to a degree that will interfere with effective listening.

ACTIVE LISTENING

Active listening is a skill that can be developed to improve the ability of the receiver to effectively hear and interpret the sender's message. Active listening consists of the receiver paying close attention to what the sender is saying and feeling and then responding, in the receiver's own words, about his or her understanding of the sender's message.

Active listening is important feedback because it allows the receiver to check his or her understanding of the sender's message. By affirming his or her understanding of the speaker's message, the receiver lessens the misunderstandings and bad feelings that may occur during their communication.

Active listening communicates the following types of messages:

- I understand what you are saying.
- I want to hear what you are telling me.
- I am paying attention and I am concerned.
- I respect you as a person.
- I understand your thoughts.
- I am not trying to either change or evaluate your message.

Active-Listening Skills

Following are some techniques that can improve your active-listening skills.

1. Look directly at the sender and maintain eye contact. Be aware of the sender's nonverbal communication. (When communicating with individuals from other cultures, take into consideration that eye contact may not always be appropriate.)

2. Focus on the sender and try not to let your mind wander.

3. Encourage the sender by nodding your head, smiling, or saying, "Uh huh," "I see," and so on. Do whatever is natural for you.

4. Pay close attention to the content of the message and the feelings of the sender, such as anger, sadness, frustration, excitement, and so on.

5. Respond by saying, in your own words, what you think the other person is communicating and feeling.

6. Begin your feedback with statements such as:

- In other words, you are feeling....
- What I hear you say is....
- As I understand, you....

Step 5: Interpreting and Understanding the Information

The fifth step in the communication process occurs when the receiver interprets the sender's message and either understands it as it was intended or does not understand it. Two major barriers to the receiver's interpreting and understanding the message of the sender are prejudgment and subjectivity.

Prejudgment: The receiver may prejudge the sender's message based on a variety of extraneous factors. Some of these include the tone, voice, accent, or appearance of the sender. Prejudging the message as good, bad, or uninteresting based on external factors will not help the receiver to understand the message as it may have been intended. The greater the understanding the receiver has of his or her own prejudices about people, things, and ideas, the more open the receiver can be to any messages he or she may hear.

Subjectivity: Being subjective is often evidenced as hearing what you want to hear rather than listening to what is being communicated. Highly subjective individuals—people who base what they hear on their own personal values—have fixed ideas. They need to interpret the message so that it fits into their frames of reference in order to make sense of it. In doing so, they will often distort the content of the message.

One way to increase your objectivity when you are listening is to be aware of the facts that are being shared without distorting them. To keep the facts clear, paraphrase what you heard to ensure that you understand the message.

Step 6: Sending Feedback

The last step in the communication process is the receiver's reaction to the sender's message. The receiver can respond in a number of ways to the sender's communication. A nonverbal expression, such as a puzzled look, may indicate the receiver's lack of understanding of the intended message; nodding the head may affirm what is being said.

Feedback works best when the receiver has already actively listened and paraphrased the sender's message. Then the sender knows that the receiver is responding to the message that was intended. The actual feedback may be as simple as saying, "I understand what you are saying," or "I agree with you."

Feedback allows the sender to check on how successful he or she has been in transferring the message. It also determines whether understanding has been achieved.

Successful teams develop effective communication processes. If the team members do not have the ability to share information, the quality of work is impeded. Effective communication is a necessary element that must be developed if teams are to thrive in the workplace.

QUICK REVIEW

Definition of Effective Communication

Effective communication is the verbal and nonverbal exchange of information between two or more people that is satisfactorily received and acted on by all parties.

The Six-Step Communication Model

In order to explain the dynamics of the communication process, a six-step communication model is presented. It is made up of the following steps:

1. Formulating the Information,

2. Converting the Information,

3. Sending the Information,

4. Receiving the Information,

5. Interpreting and Understanding the Information, and

6. Sending Feedback.

Formulating the Information

The three factors to consider before deciding to communicate information are as follows:

- Content,

- Clarity, and
- Timing.

Converting the Information

The three symbolic categories in the communication process are as follows:

- Body language,
- Vocal expression, and
- Words or language.

Sending the Information

To effectively send information, the following questions should be answered by the sender before the communication begins:

- Is the form of expression being used appropriate for the receiver?
- Is too much or too little information being communicated?
- Is the receiver paying attention?

Receiving the Information

To effectively receive information, the following questions should be answered by the receiver before the communication begins:

- Am I paying attention?
- Am I listening in an active or passive manner?

Interpreting and Understanding the Information

Two major barriers to the receiver's interpreting and understanding the message of the sender are as follows:

- Prejudgment, and
- Subjectivity.

Sending Feedback

Feedback works best when the receiver has already actively listened and paraphrased the sender's message. Then the sender knows that the receiver is responding to the message that was intended. The actual feedback may be as simple as saying, "I understand what you are saying," or "I agree with you."

4

TEAM DEVELOPMENT

Once a team has been formed and assessed and has developed effective communication skills, team development is the next challenge. The manager or team leader must be prepared to guide the team through a developmental process that is common to all newly formed groups.

Chapter 4 does the following:

- Defines team development;
- Describes the stages of team development; and
- Discusses what team leaders can do to facilitate the stages of team development.

DEFINITION OF TEAM DEVELOPMENT

When a group of individuals first is formed into a team, members' roles and interactions are unclear. Individuals may tend to act as observers while they try to decide what is expected of them. Gradually, the process of "team development" occurs, as team members learn their roles, establish ways of doing things, and become acquainted with team issues, pressures, goals, etc. The process of team development consists of five relatively predictable stages.

STAGES OF TEAM DEVELOPMENT

Teams generally can be categorized as those that work well and those that do not. A team that works well has developed from a collection of individuals to a cohesive, functional unit by completing the stages of team development (Kormanski & Mozenter, 1991; Tuckman & Jenson, 1977) described on the following page.

- Stage I: Orientation or Forming,
- Stage II: Conflict or Storming,
- Stage III: Collaboration or Norming,
- Stage IV: Productivity or Performing, and
- Stage V: Changing or Transforming.

Each stage is unique and each stage is experienced by all teams that develop into cohesive, functional units.

Stage I: Orientation or Forming

The behaviors expressed by team members in this first stage are initially polite and superficial. While introductions are made, team members make decisions about the other team members. They try to assess which team members have needs similar to theirs and which have different needs.

Sometimes confusion and anxiety are experienced as different styles and different needs surface within the team. At this point, team members attempt to establish safe patterns for interacting with one another and basic criteria for team membership.

Each member is working at varying levels of intensity on the issue of inclusion or belonging to the team. Some questions raised during this first stage are as follows:

- Do I wish to be included with these people?
- Will they accept me as I am?
- What is the price to join this team and am I willing to pay it?

This first stage reflects a strong dependence on formal leadership. As team members experience confusion and anxiety, they look to whatever leadership already exists within the team.

The first stage may be smooth and pleasant or intense and frustrating for some or all team members, depending on the similarities in style, needs, and the tolerance for ambiguity that exist in the team.

Team leaders can facilitate team members through the first stage by following these guidelines:

- Provide structure to the team by assisting in task and role clarification.
- Encourage participation by all members.
- Share relevant information with the team.
- Facilitate learning about one another.
- Encourage open communication among team members.

Stage II: Conflict or Storming

When a common level of expectation is developed, the team will move into the conflict or storming stage of development. Conflict cannot be avoided. This is a difficult and crucial stage. It deals with power and decision making, two issues that are important to the future functioning of the team.

In this stage, team members begin to challenge differences in an attempt to regain their individuality and influence. Some team members may start to respond to the perceived demands of the team's task with a full range of emotions. Regardless of how clear the task or structure of the team is, team members will react and strike out at the designated team leader, as well as any emerging team leaders within the team. The members' actions may either take the form of direct attacks or covert nonsupport. Team members are working through their own needs to be in sufficient control and to have some sense of direction.

The leadership issue is one of counterdependence or attempting to resolve the felt dependency of Stage I by reacting negatively to any leadership behavior that is evident. Until team members break out of this stage and begin initiating independent and interdependent behavior, they will remain stuck in Stage II or return to Stage I.

As team members begin to create and establish acceptable decision-making processes within the team, they will cycle into Stage III. The activity and skills gained in the second stage are essential for the team to proceed. The more aware the team is of what it has accomplished in this stage, the faster the team will evolve and develop in the future.

Team leaders can facilitate team members through Stage II by following these guidelines:

- Assist the team members in establishing norms that support the communication of their different points of view.

- Discuss how the team will make decisions.

- Encourage members to share their ideas about issues.

- Facilitate conflict resolution.

Stage III: Collaboration or Norming

Once the team members have completed the first two stages, the team can finally pull together as a real team, not merely as a collection of individuals. At this stage the team becomes a cohesive unit, and the team members begin to negotiate roles and processes for accomplishing their tasks. Functional relationships are explored and established by the members in spite of their differences. The team is working together collaboratively. With the accomplishment of some goals, team members may gain and share insights into the factors that contribute to or hinder their success.

Team members are now committed to working with other team members. Functional relationships have developed between members. Leadership issues are resolved through interdependent behavior. Tasks are accomplished by recognizing the unique talents in the team. Trust, the active ingredient in team cohesiveness, evolves.

Team leaders can facilitate team members through Stage III by following these guidelines:

- Talk openly about issues and the team members' concerns.

- Encourage the team members to give feedback.

- Assign tasks for consensus decision making.

- Delegate to team members as much as possible.

Stage IV: Productivity or Performing

This stage is the payoff for working through the first three stages. At this stage, the members have learned to work together in a fully functioning team. Members now have the skills to define tasks, work out relationships, manage conflict, and work toward producing results. Stage IV is the most harmonious and productive stage of the team's life. The team has a sense of its own identity, and members are committed to the team and its goals.

Team leaders can facilitate team members through Stage IV by following these guidelines:

- Jointly set goals that are challenging to all team members.
- Look for ways to increase the team's chances to excel.
- Question traditional ways of behaving.
- Develop an ongoing assessment of the team.
- Recognize each individual contribution.
- Develop members to their fullest potential through coaching and the use of feedback.

THE PROCESS IS SEQUENTIAL

As in any development process, the development-cycle for teams also has pitfalls. Inattention to possible problems may result in more frustration and anxiety than is needed in any respective stage. If no learning or insight is gained, team members will wonder, "Why are we doing all this again?" Team members must be attentive to their process and learn from it.

Teams may also regress to a previous stage before completing the full cycle. There are a number of reasons for this:

- Any changes in the composition of the team necessitates returning to Stage I.

- A change in team leadership necessitates returning to Stage I.

- Inattention to the needed activities in a stage will require, sooner or later, a return to that stage.

Stage V: Changing or Transforming

Any time the team's goal has been achieved, the team is faced with transforming. Transforming can take one of two paths: Redefinition of or establishment of a new goal or structure, or disengagement or termination of the team. The team must decide on the next step or it will proceed down a frustrating path. The natural tendency for any team that has successfully achieved a full cycle is to attempt to remain intact. The shared experiences—with all of their successes and good feelings—bond the members of the team together. If the team is to continue with new members, it will cycle through the five stages of development again. However, some teams must end when their tasks are completed. It is important at this point to honor the *team's* accomplishments, celebrate the *members'* personal and mutual growth and accomplishments, and emphasize learnings that members can take with them to future teams. Appropriate closure frees the members to form new alliances.

The team leader should make sure that all team members understand the team-development process. The dynamics that occur in the storming phase, such as conflict, are present in all teams. When team members recognize that they are operating in a structured environment, they will better understand their own feelings and deal more effectively with the behaviors of others. It is beneficial for a team to realize that teams progress through predictable stages. Being able to recognize what stage it is in can help the team to deal with current issues and prevent frustrations.

References

Kormanski, C.L., & Mozenter, A. (1991). A model of team building. In J.W. Pfeiffer & A.C. Ballew (Eds.), *Theories and models in applied behavioral science.* (Vol. 3, Management/Leadership). San Diego, CA: Pfeiffer & Company.

Tuckman, B.W., & Jenson, M.A. (1977). Stages of small group development revisited. *Group and Organization Studies, 2*(4), 419-427.

QUICK REVIEW

Definition of Team Development

When a group of individuals first is formed into a team, members' roles and interactions are unclear. Individuals may tend to act as observers while they try to decide what is expected of them. Gradually, the process of "team development" occurs, as team members learn their roles, establish ways of doing things, and become acquainted with team issues, pressures, goals, etc. The process of team development consists of five relatively predictable stages.

Stages of Team Development

New ongoing teams generally go through five major stages of development:

- Stage I: Orientation or Forming,
- Stage II: Conflict or Storming,
- Stage III: Collaboration or Norming,
- Stage IV: Productivity or Performing, and
- Stage V: Changing or Transforming.

Each stage is unique and each stage is experienced by all teams that develop into cohesive, functional units.

Stage I: The major issue in the first stage is members' inclusion into the team. Team members have a strong dependency on formal leadership.

Stage II: The major issue in the second stage is conflict. Team members will challenge the formal leadership in an attempt to regain individuality and influence.

Stage III: The major issue in the third stage is norming. The team members can finally pull together as a real team, not merely as a collection of individuals. The team becomes a cohesive unit, and the team members begin to negotiate roles for accomplishing their tasks.

Stage IV: The major issue in the fourth stage is performing. Stage IV is the most harmonious and productive stage of the team's life. The team has a sense of its own identity, and members are committed to the team and its goals.

Stage V: The major issue in the final stage is transforming. Any time the team has reached its intended outcome, the team members must redefine or establish a new purpose for their team or terminate the team.

5

TEAM-MEMBER ROLES

When individuals come together to form a team, a number of dynamics occur simultaneously. Some team members are very goal oriented while others spend time working on interpersonal relationships. Team members often test issues that concern them, such as influence, expertise, conflict management, decision making, and roles. Such testing is a necessary part of effective team development.

Chapter 5 does the following:

- Defines team-member roles;
- Describes the differences between task and process roles;
- Describes seven task roles;
- Describes four positive process roles;
- Describes five negative process roles; and
- Describes methods for managing negative process behaviors.

DEFINITION OF TEAM MEMBER ROLES

One aspect of team dynamics is the way in which members interact in order to carry out their tasks. As team development progresses, members settle into individual "roles" by mutual consent. Such roles include both *task* and *process* aspects of the team's interaction.

TASK AND PROCESS ROLES

There are two important dynamics to consider when examining group-member roles: task and process.

Some of the task and process roles team members perform are more typical of everyday interpersonal experiences, and other behaviors are specific to teams. Yet, for teams to maximize their performance, it is important that each team member understand and play the appropriate role at the right time. Building an effective team is dependent on how the relationships between the dynamics of task and process are managed.

Task Roles Are Concerned with "What" and "Why"

The task dynamic refers to what a team must do to achieve its goal. Task dynamics are the "what" and "why" issues of the team's work. They include activities that facilitate the completion of a team's task. Task roles include establishing vision, objectives, implementation strategies, and the functional roles of team members. These drive the team toward its ultimate goal.

Process Roles Are Concerned with "How"

The process dynamic refers to the personal and the social needs of the team members that contribute to a sense of team cohesiveness. It is the "how" dynamic that the team uses to facilitate task accomplishment.

The process dynamic includes such factors as which team members talk, how much they talk, and who talks to whom. This area of team member interaction seldom receives direct attention, yet it is the area that creates the most team problems. Effective facilitation in this area is key to maintaining high team morale, which influences team success.

Effective team members combine their abilities to manage the relationship between task and process issues. It is important that all team members understand and attend to both of these dynamics.

To gain a better understanding of the differences between task and process dynamics, we need to examine task and process behaviors.

TASK ROLES

The task roles played by team members can either facilitate or hinder team interaction. The two most common task roles in teams are the "giver" and the "seeker" of information.

Giving Information

The most common form of communication between team members is when individuals express opinions or facts in one-way communication. This exchange of information or opinion by a member is usually given in the context of offering data or information. The team member playing the role of information giver will be seen as either helping or hindering the process, depending on what information is shared. If this role is played by several team members, it may be an indication that members are listening to one another.

To manage this form of communication, the team leader or the manager must ensure a balance between the free flow of information and an orderly process that ensures each member an opportunity to be heard.

Seeking Information

Another role played by most team members is that of information seeker. In this role, members ask questions, request facts, ask for suggestions, and seek opinions from other team members. This role is important because it helps to clarify discussion topics. However, if this is the predominant role played by many team members, it may indicate that the team is uninformed or overly dependent on other team members or the team leader.

To manage this form of communication, the manager or team leader must ensure a balance between attentive consideration and active participation by all team members.

Other Task Roles

Giving and seeking information are only two of a team's task roles. Other task roles that are important for team members to perform are as follows:

- Initiating,
- Standard setting,
- Clarifying,
- Summarizing, and
- Consensus testing.

These task roles are less familiar to team members, but are important for effective team interaction and decision making. These roles usually must be taught to team members.

Initiating

In the initiating role, the manager or team leader may propose a task or goal, define a problem, or suggest a procedure. Although initiating is often seen as the manager's or team leader's role, it is important that other team members take responsibility for initiating tasks or goals in their areas of expertise or in areas they consider to be important.

Standard Setting

In the standard-setting role, the manager or a team leader establishes team norms and behavioral limits. These team standards sometimes are referred to as the "rules of the road." Standards such as "be on time for team meetings," "only one member can talk at a time," and "decision making by consensus" are some examples. The standards or rules can be established by the manager or team leader; the critical factor is that everyone accept the rules and participate in their enforcement.

Clarifying

In the clarifying role, the team members can interpret and elaborate on ideas or suggestions, define and redefine terms, and paraphrase or restate other team members' opinions. This role is important because it assists the team members in understanding the team's topic of conversation.

Summarizing

In the summarizing role, the team members can restate ideas, opinions, or suggestions in a systematic fashion. Summarizing provides the team members with clarity about an issue, decision, or conclusion. This role is often played by the manager or the team leader, but in a mature team, it can be played by any member.

Consensus Testing

In the consensus-testing role, any team member can check on the team's position through polling or formal voting. This process is important for making decisions, resolving conflict issues, and formulating positions. The role often is played by the manager or the team leader, but in a mature team, it can be played by any member.

POSITIVE PROCESS ROLES

In comparison to task roles, which focus on the "what" and "why" issues within the team, process roles focus on the team's needs concerning commitment, dependence, and involvement. These team needs are more emotional in nature and relate to self-esteem and individual ego needs.

Process behaviors, like task roles, can either hinder or facilitate the team's interaction. The behaviors that we learn as part of our socialization can be viewed either positively or negatively by other team members. Fortunately, role behaviors that facilitate team dynamics can be learned and effectively practiced in teams. Similarly, the negative behaviors can be minimized using the same learning process.

Supporting and Encouraging

The most common positive role that team members play is that of supporting and encouraging other team members. This role is demonstrated by being friendly, warm, and responsive to other team members' contributions. The result of this role is the development of a climate of support and trust that facilitates team effectiveness. Understanding the importance of recognizing another member's contributions, even when one might disagree, is a critical part of the role.

Encouraging and supporting behaviors can be both verbal and nonverbal. An example of verbal support is when one team member states his or her agreement with another team member or acknowledges that team member's contribution to the team. Nonverbal support includes eye contact and positive facial expressions.

Although team members may agree with other members' ideas or opinions, they often do not express their support openly. Team members can learn encouraging and supporting behaviors through awareness and skill practice.

Harmonizing and Mediating

Another positive role some team members innately play is that of harmonizer or mediator. Harmonizing and mediating behaviors are demonstrated when members offer to negotiate, admit error, or modify an opinion in the interest of team cohesion. Maintaining group cohesion is a critical aspect of the role. Team members can learn and effectively utilize harmonizing and mediating behaviors through awareness and practice.

Gatekeeping

The gatekeeping role is not common in everyday human interactions. Gatekeeping encompasses a set of skills that are important to effective team interaction. This role involves helping to keep communication channels open among team members and taking interest in other team members' opinions and feelings.

Because some team members are more assertive than others, the gatekeeping role ensures that the less assertive members receive an opportunity to express their opinions and that the more assertive ones do not monopolize the discussion.

Team members can learn these skills through training and skill practice. However, it is important to recognize that gatekeeping behaviors are assertive by nature; a team member acting in the gatekeeping role must often redirect or even stop the flow of communication.

Challenging

Challenging is considered a positive role. The skill that is required for performing this role is the ability to deal directly with disruptive team members in a calm but assertive manner. The challenging role can include the ability to give honest and relevant feedback in a timely manner.

The skill set for the challenging role can be learned when practiced. However, it must be noted that practicing this skill is difficult because of the potential risk of a negative response by the members being confronted. Challenging can be done in a gentle and nonthreatening manner when there is trust and support within the team.

NEGATIVE PROCESS BEHAVIORS

The following are five negative process behaviors.

Withdrawing

The behaviors associated with this role include acting passive or indifferent, daydreaming, doodling, whispering while others talk, and wandering from the subject of discussion.

Blocking

The behaviors associated with this role include wandering from the subject of discussion, citing personal experiences unrelated to the problem, arguing too much on a point, and rejecting expressed ideas without consideration.

Joking

The behaviors associated with this role include excessive playing around, telling jokes, mimicking other members, and other playful behavior that interferes with the team's work.

Dominating

The behaviors associated with this role include excessive talking, interrupting others, trying to gain status by criticizing or blaming others, showing open hostility toward other team members, and deflating the status of others.

Self-Seeking

The behaviors associated with this role include putting one's personal needs before the team's needs, trying to induce other team members to be sympathetic to one's misfortunes, deploring one's situation, and disparaging one's own ideas to gain support.

HANDLING NEGATIVE PROCESS BEHAVIORS

Each team member will probably play both positive and negative process roles at some time. However, the success of any team will be determined by how these process roles are managed.

When team members continue to exhibit negative process behaviors, the leader or other team members must take immediate action to curb these behaviors, using one of the following approaches.

Individual Counseling

A team leader, facilitator, or team member should meet with the disruptive team member in a one-on-one setting. During the meeting, it is important that the disruptive member receive specific feedback about his or her negative behaviors.

Confronting the Individual With the Team

If individual counseling is ineffective, a team leader, facilitator, or team member may decide to confront a disruptive team member in a team meeting. This action is important because other members can provide additional, specific feedback to the disruptive member about the effects of his or her negative behavior and also provide him or her with needed support.

Dismissing the Team Member

When all else fails, the team leader or facilitator may have to ask the disruptive member to leave the team. Although it is unusual to terminate a member involuntarily, there may be a few cases that warrant this type of unilateral action. Highly disruptive team members should be asked to leave the team. It is important that all team members recognize why the member is being asked to leave and agree with the decision.

Successful teams have members who play a variety of positive task and process roles. The more these positive roles are shared among members, the greater the buy-in and commitment to the overall team goals and objectives.

QUICK REVIEW

Definition of Team-Member Roles

One aspect of team dynamics is the way in which members interact in order to carry out their tasks. As team development progresses, members settle into individual "roles" by mutual consent. Such roles include both *task* and *process* aspects of the team's interaction.

Task and Process Roles

Task: The task dynamic refers to what a team must do to achieve its goal. It is the "what" and "why" of the team's work.

Process: The process dynamic refers to the personal and social needs of team members that contribute to a sense of team cohesiveness.

Task Roles

The task roles played by team members can either facilitate or hinder team interaction. The task roles are as follows:

- Giving information,
- Seeking information,
- Initiating,
- Standard setting,
- Clarifying,
- Summarizing, and
- Consensus testing.

Positive Process Roles

Positive process roles focus on the team's need for commitment, dependence, and involvement. These needs are more emotional in nature and related to self-esteem and individual ego needs. The roles are as follows:

- Supporting and encouraging,
- Harmonizing and mediating,
- Gatekeeping, and
- Challenging.

Negative Process Behaviors

The following are negative process behaviors.

- Withdrawing,
- Blocking,
- Joking,
- Dominating, and
- Self-Seeking.

Handling Negative Process Behaviors

When team members continue to exhibit negative process behaviors, the leader or a team member must take immediate action to curb these behaviors using one of the following approaches.

- Individual counseling,
- Confronting the individual with the team, and
- Dismissing the team member.

6

DECISION MAKING

Once a team has learned about task and process roles, those skills can be used to increase the team's ability to make quality decisions. However, without a systematic process for dealing with team issues, time and resources are often wasted. The team now needs to learn about and understand the dynamics of the decision-making process.

Chapter 6 does the following:

- Defines decision making;
- Describes an eight-step decision-making model;
- Discusses five decision-making procedures;
- Examines four advantages to participatory decision making; and
- Tells how to implement the decisions.

DEFINITION OF DECISION MAKING

Decision making is the process by which individuals or groups arrive at a decision, judgment, or conclusion through a process of deliberation.

A DECISION-MAKING MODEL

Once a team has thoroughly discussed an issue on its agenda and is ready to make a decision, there are a variety of ways in which the decision can be made. When a team is ready to make a decision, it is important that the team be clear about what decision must be made and *how* the decision will be made.

To be clear about the decision that must be made, the team should follow the eight steps below.

1. *Clarify the purpose of the decision.* Any decision-making process must begin with a clear analysis of the factors surrounding the decision and the relationship of that decision to other decisions.

2. *Establish criteria by considering the results that the team wants.* The criteria represent the basis on which the team will actually decide. In a team situation, the team leader should make certain that the team members who are going to be influenced by the decision have the opportunity to provide input.

3. *Separate the criteria by classifying them into two categories: limiting factors and desirable features.* Limiting factors include criteria such as the budget and time restrictions that any option must meet. Desirable features should be listed according to their priority and include items such as location and access.

4. *Generate options by weighing the limiting factors of each of the desirable options.* Make a list of acceptable options.

5. *Compare options.* Collect data on each one. This will help the team to measure the satisfaction on each criterion.

6. *Identify the risks of each option.* Do each one separately and determine the concerns that the team has about the ultimate effects of each option.

7. *Assess the risks of each option by ranking them.* Rank each of the options according to probability (that is, on a scale of 10 to 1, where 10 = likely and 1 = unlikely).

8. *Make the decision.* The team should make a decision using one of the following procedures: authority decision, minority decision, majority-rule decision, consensus, or unanimity. A consensus decision or unanimity achieves the most buy-in from team members. However, sometimes one of the other types of decision is more appropriate, e.g., when expediency is more important than buy-in.

FIVE DECISION-MAKING PROCEDURES

The five decision-making procedures that can be used by a team are explained in the following text.

Decision by Authority

This decision-making procedure occurs when the highest ranking authority within a team makes a unilateral decision. In effect, the leader has decision making and veto power. This decision-making method is appropriate when the manager or team leader is held completely accountable by the organization for the team's final decision. There is a story about President Lincoln taking a vote among his cabinet members concerning a vital presidential issue. The vote was twelve to one against Lincoln, but Lincoln's one vote (he was the ultimate authority) carried the issue.

Decision by Minority

This procedure occurs when a minority within

AUTHORS' NOTE

If a team leader wants the team to buy into a decision and achieve high levels of motivation to support a decision, it is best not to use the decision-by-authority procedure.

a team exerts its influence over the majority of team members and carries the decision. The subgroup, in effect, has decision making and veto power. This decision-making method is appropriate when the minority members have the expert knowledge and feel strongly about the issue (especially if the majority members do not) and when the minority is most affected by the decision outcome.

AUTHORS' NOTE

Decision making by minority influence can create resentment and hostility among team members if a strong-willed and vocal minority pushes or "railroads" a decision that the majority of the group opposes.

Decision by Majority

This procedure occurs when a majority of team members agree with the issues. The majority-rule procedure is the most popular decision-making procedure because it is based on democratic principles. It is a political principle that a majority, constituted by 50 percent plus one member of an organized group, will have the power to make decisions binding on the entire group. This is an appropriate decision-making procedure

---

AUTHORS' NOTE

In a majority-rule decision, only the majority of team members are likely to be satisfied with the outcome. The members in the minority are forced to accept a decision that they oppose. In extreme cases, the tyranny of the majority may force hardship on other team members. The majority decision-making procedure is not the best one to use if a manager or team leader wants commitment and "buy in" from all team members.

when time is limited and when the consequences of the decision will not have a negative impact on the minority team members who are not voting in favor of the decision.

Decision by Consensus

Decision by consensus means finding a proposal that is acceptable enough so that all team members can support it to some degree. Every team member has veto power in this procedure. For a team to use the consensus decision-making procedure effectively, it must have sufficient time to make a decision, active participation by all members, a creative climate that supports team decision-making by consensus, and mutual trust, respect, and commitment by all team members.

Consensus decision making provides a win-win solution that reflects the thinking of all team members, increases commitment to the implementation of the decision, and provides a climate of empowerment.

AUTHORS' NOTE

For consensus decision making to be effective, there must be sufficient time for each team member to share his or her ideas. If the time for making a decision is limited or team members are not skilled in the appropriate consensus decision-making techniques, a decision will be difficult to reach.

Decision by Unanimity

This decision-making procedure occurs when all members of a team are in full agreement with a decision. The unanimity decision-making procedure is often confused with consensus decision making. The team should make a unanimous decision when the issue is so important that it is necessary for all team members to be in complete accord. One example of the unanimity decision-making procedure can be found in the United States' legal system in the form of a jury.

AUTHORS' NOTE

Unanimity is very difficult to achieve in any group, regardless of the groups' experience. It should be attempted only when the outcome of a decision is critical to each team member.

ADVANTAGES OF PARTICIPATORY DECISION MAKING

The procedures presented for making decisions can all be participatory, even decision by authority. Members must interact to produce an outcome.

Decision by consensus, however, is the most practical participatory decision-making procedure and produces the greatest number of win-win solutions for all team members. Four of the advantages of consensus decision making are presented below.

Increased Information and Knowledge

By effectively using team resources, which are all of the members, more facts and opinions can be considered before the team makes a decision.

Increased Diversity of Views

By allowing the team members' different points of view to be surfaced, a greater diversity of approaches and options can be considered by the team.

Increased Acceptance of the Solution

When team members are affected by any type of decision and are instrumental in implementing it, they will be more likely to fully accept the decision.

Increased Legitimacy

Because the consensus decision-making process is consistent with democratic ideals, it will be perceived as being the most legitimate way to make difficult decisions.

IMPLEMENTING DECISIONS

Some teams make many decisions that are never implemented. Therefore, managers or team leaders will need to include an implementation strategy when any type of decision is made. Without an implementation strategy, follow-through is less likely to occur. The strategy can be as specific as developing a step-by-step action plan or as general as simply assigning the implementation of the decision to a team member. In any case, the implementation of all decisions requires accountability.

Successful teams develop a successful decision-making process. Without this ability, teams will never move beyond the discussion of problems. A team that cannot make decisions is of no use to anyone.

QUICK REVIEW

Definition of Decision Making

Decision making is the process by which individuals or groups arrive at a decision, judgment, or conclusion through a process of deliberation.

A Decision-Making Model

When team members meet to make decisions, it is important that they:

- Be clear about what decision must be made.
- Be clear about how the decision will be made.

To be clear about what decision must be made, the eight steps listed below will facilitate the decision-making process:

1. Clarify the purpose of the decision.

2. Establish criteria by considering the results that the team wants.

3. Separate the criteria by classifying them into two categories: limiting factors and desirable features.

4. Generate options by weighing the limiting factors of each of the desirable options.

5. Compare options.

6. Identify the risks of each option.

7. Assess the risks of each option by ranking them.

8. Make the decision.

Decision-Making Procedures

Team members should use one of the following decision-making procedures to arrive at a decision.

- Decision by authority,
- Decision by minority,
- Decision by majority,
- Decision by consensus, or
- Decision by unanimity.

Advantages of Participatory Decision Making

Four of the advantages of participatory decision making are listed below.

1. Increased information and knowledge,

2. Increased diversity of views,

3. Increased acceptance of the solution, and

4. Increased legitimacy.

Implementing Decisions

Efficient teams develop a successful decision-making process. Without this ability, teams will never move beyond the discussion of problems. A team that cannot make decisions is of no use to anyone in the organization.

Things to Consider When Making a Decision

- Be clear about *what* the team wants to decide.

- Be clear about *how* the team is going to make the decision.
- Be clear about *who* will be ultimately accountable for implementing the decision.
- Just do it...make the decision.

7

RESOLVING TEAM CONFLICT

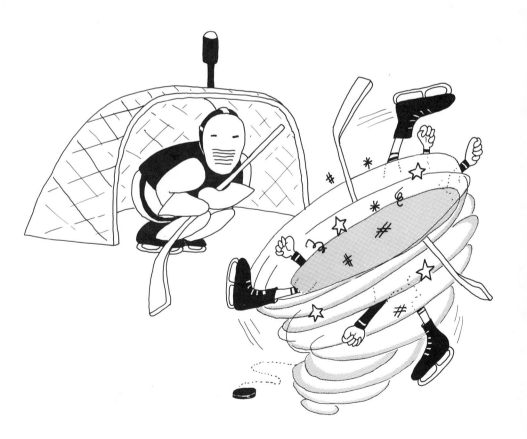

One natural by-product of any type of decision making is conflict. Conflict can be attributed to a number of factors such as a team's stage of development; the team members' different opinions, values, decision-making styles; and miscommunication. However, the team's ability to manage and resolve conflicts is critical if it is to function at a high level.

Chapter 7 does the following:

- Defines conflict;
- Presents three views of conflict;
- Examines six causes of conflict;
- Identifies five conflict-management strategies;
- Discusses when to use the strategies; and
- Describes a six-step process for dealing with team conflict.

DEFINITION OF CONFLICT

Conflict can be defined as an emotional disturbance resulting from a clash of opposing points of view or from an inability to manage those points of view with realistic or moral considerations.

Conflict in teams results from competitive, opposing, or divergent ideas that prevent team members from reaching an agreement. The inability of team members to reach an agreement may be attributed to either the means or ends needed to produce an outcome. If the conflict goes unresolved, it can lead to disharmony and low morale within the team, resulting in poor team performance.

THREE VIEWS OF CONFLICT

To gain a better understanding of the meaning of conflict, we will examine three different points of view that relate to conflict in groups. It is important that the managers or team leaders understand the nature of conflict and how to manage it.

Traditional Perspective

The traditional perspective views conflict as dysfunctional and caused by poor communication and lack of trust and openness within the team. From this perspective, the best way to manage conflict is to avoid it at all cost.

Human Relations Perspective

The human relations perspective views conflict as a natural and an inevitable part of the interpersonal experience. Because conflict cannot be avoided, it should be managed effectively.

Interactionist Perspective

The interactionist perspective views conflict as a potentially useful part of the interpersonal experience that should be allowed because a harmonious and overly cooperative team can become apathetic and nonresponsive to change.

AUTHORS' NOTE

It is important to recognize that all three perspectives can be shared by team members at any point in time. The key to effective conflict management is managing the delicate balance between the freedom of individual dissent and the cohesiveness of team solidarity. It also is important to recognize and understand the different conflict-management strategies that team members can use.

CAUSES OF CONFLICT

To better understand the nature of conflict, we will examine the various perspectives regarding the causes of conflict.

Personality Differences

It is likely that there will be personality differences among members. Such differences can be as simple as physical appearance or language style or as complex as how members make decisions or whether individuals are more extraverted or introverted.

Value Differences

Team members may express divergent points of view based on strongly held personal values. This may lead to conflict if, for example, a team member values competition over collaboration. When a member is more concerned about a personal win than about working as a team, the team will have a difficult time working to produce a win-win solution.

Differences in Perspectives

Often, team members have different perspectives because of their different backgrounds, experiences, skills, and job positions. This should be viewed as a team strength, not a problem.

Differences in Goals

Some team members may have personal objectives or goals that conflict with the team's goal. These are often called "hidden agendas" or undisclosed personal desires. The problem is that such goals may need to be obtained at the expense of other team members or the team.

Differences in Departmental Allegiance

Some team members may report to many department managers in the organization. Conflicts may arise from issues based on departmental affiliations.

Cultural Differences

Some teams are made up of individuals from diverse backgrounds. If the manager or the team leader lacks the knowledge and skill to manage the differences in the team, this can lead to conflict with a possible outcome of poor team performance and low morale. A team leader's inability to manage cultural differences in the workplace can be a major cause of conflict.

AUTHORS' NOTE

Conflict can exist in a team without being openly expressed. This can be expressed through lack of cooperation, resistance to new ideas, or illogical thinking. This is the most insidious type of conflict and it must be surfaced and managed immediately or the schism it creates will be too hard to control over time. When conflict arises, the team leader should deal with it as soon as possible.

CONFLICT-MANAGEMENT STRATEGIES

The figure shown represents a process by Kenneth W. Thomas and Ralph H. Kilmann for assessing an individual's behavior in conflict situations. Using two dimensions—cooperativeness (the degree to which one party attempts to satisfy the other party's concerns) and assertiveness (the degree to which one party attempts to satisfy his or her own concerns)–five conflict orientations can be identified:

- Competition (assertive and uncooperative),
- Collaboration (assertive and cooperative),
- Avoidance (unassertive and uncooperative),
- Accommodation (unassertive and cooperative), and
- Compromising (midrange on both assertive and cooperative).

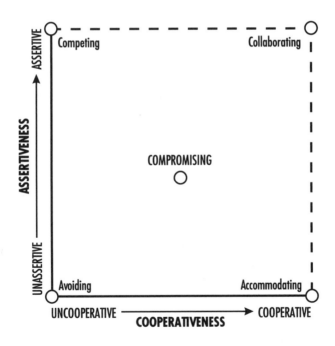

Adapted from the model of conflict presented by Kenneth Thomas in M.D. Dunnette (Ed.), *Handbook of Industrial and Organizational Psychology.* New York: John Wiley & Sons, 1976. Used with permission of current copyright owner, Marvin D. Dunnette.

Competition

Competition occurs when a team member seeks to achieve a goal or further an interest at the expense of others. In the United States, this win-lose approach is supported by a cultural value that strongly supports winning over losing as the only way to manage conflict.

Collaboration

Collaboration occurs when team members work toward dealing with the concerns of all members. This contributes to a mutually beneficial outcome. When collaborating, members are concerned with solving problems and clarifying differences. When team members collaborate, they are able to consider the full range of alternatives, similarities, and differences; become more clearly focused; and resolve problems more satisfactorily. Collaboration is a win-win approach to resolving conflict.

AUTHORS' NOTE

No one conflict-resolution approach is appropriate to all situations. However, most individuals use a variety of approaches to resolve conflict.

Some research suggests that each person has a preferred style of conflict resolution. A conflict-resolution style tends to be used consistently regardless of the situation. Often, an individual's mode of conflict resolution can be predicted based on his or her personality.

Avoidance

Avoidance occurs when a member reacts to conflict by withdrawing or by suppressing the conflict. The member's withdrawal can be either physical or psychological.

Accommodation

Accommodation occurs when team members are willing to place their opponent's interests above their own. This is often self-sacrificing behavior.

Compromise

Compromising occurs when each team member must give up something of value to help resolve the conflict. In compromising, there is no clear winner or loser. Each member yields something in order to reach an agreement or resolution.

WHEN TO USE THE FIVE CONFLICT STRATEGIES

CONFLICT-RESOLUTION APPROACH	APPROPRIATE SITUATION
COMPETITION	1. When quick, decisive action is necessary.
	2. When the issues are important and unpopular actions need to be implemented.
	3. When the issues are vital to the organization's welfare and you know you are right.
	4. Against people who take advantage of noncompetitive behavior.
	5. When other options are not possible.
COLLABORATION	1. When you need to find an integrative solution and both sets of concerns are too important to be compromised.
	2. When your objective is to learn.
	3. When you need to merge insights from people with different perspectives.
	4. When you want to gain commitment by incorporating concerns into a consensus decision.
	5. When you want to work through feelings that have interfered with a relationship.

CONFLICT-RESOLUTION APPROACH	APPROPRIATE SITUATION
AVOIDANCE	1. When an issue is trivial or more important issues are pressing.
	2. When you see that there is no chance to satisfy your major concerns.
	3. When you need to let people cool down and regain perspective.
	4. When you need more time to gather information.
	5. When others can resolve the conflict more effectively.
ACCOMMODATION	1. When you find that you are wrong.
	2. When you want to show your reasonableness.
	3. When issues are more important to others than yourself.
	4. When you want to build social support for later use.
	5. When you want to minimize your losses.
	6. When you want to allow subordinates to develop by learning from mistakes.

CONFLICT-RESOLUTION APPROACH	APPROPRIATE SITUATION
COMPROMISE	1. When goals are important but not worth the effort of disruption.
	2. When opponents with equal power are committed to different means to a similar end.
	3. When you want to achieve temporary settlements to complex issues.
	4. When you want to arrive at an expedient solution under time pressure.
	5. As a backup when collaboration or competition is not working.

Team members vary in their ability to use the five conflict-resolution strategies. Some people are capable of using all five conflict-resolution strategies. However, most people may rely on some strategies more than others.

AUTHORS' NOTE

The most desirable conflict-resolution strategy in groups is collaboration. Collaboration calls for members to work together in an atmosphere of trust, mutual respect, and commitment that supports effective teamwork.

To manage team conflict effectively, team members should understand their own conflict-management preferences. The more aware team members are of the different conflict strategies, the better prepared they will be to handle team conflict.

SIX STEPS TO MANAGING TEAM CONFLICT

When team members have a thorough understanding of their preferred conflict-resolution strategies, they can use the following six-step, win-win strategy to manage team conflict effectively.

1. Clarify: What is the conflict?

Team members should ask for information about the other members' view. A dialogue should continue until both points of view are understood.

2. Goal: What is the common goal?

Team members should try to find common goals. They should determine the other members' preferred outcome. They should then find common ground that all members can agree on.

3. Options: What are some options?

Team members should discuss their ideas with the other members to assist them in meeting their goals. They should ask one another for suggestions and explore all options.

4. Remove Barriers: What are the barriers? What would happen if the barriers were removed?

Team members should define the things that can and cannot be changed. They should remove one barrier at a time to reach agreement. Team members should ask, "If we could have the outcome we both desired, what would it be?"

5. Agree: What meets the needs of both parties?

Team members should settle on a solution that everyone can accept.

6. Acknowledge: What is the solution?

Team members should recognize the win-win solution. They should make sure that all parties understand what the solution means to them. Team members should grant credit where credit is due.

Conflict is constructive when it improves the quality of decisions, stimulates creativity and innovation, encourages interest and curiosity among team members, provides the medium through which problems can be discussed and tensions released, and fosters an environment of self-evaluation and change. The evidence suggests that conflict can improve the quality of decision making by allowing all points—particularly those that are different or held by a minority—to be weighed. Conflict is an antidote for "group think." It does not allow the team to passively accept decisions that may be based on weak assumptions or inadequate consideration of relevant alternatives. Conflict challenges the status quo and furthers the creation of new ideas; it promotes reassessment of team goals and activities and increases the probability that the team will respond to change.

QUICK REVIEW

Definition of Conflict

Conflict can be defined as an emotional disturbance resulting from a clash of opposing points of view or from an inability to manage those points of view with realistic or moral considerations.

Three Views of Conflict

It is important to understand the nature of conflict and how to manage it. This chapter presents:

- The traditional perspective,
- The human relations perspective, and
- The interactionist perspective.

Causes of Conflict

To better understand conflict, we need to examine its causes. The following six are discussed.

- Personality differences,
- Value differences,
- Differences in perspective,
- Differences in goals,
- Differences in departmental allegiance, and
- Cultural differences.

Conflict Management Strategies

The five conflict strategies are given on the following page.

1. Competition,

2. Collaboration,

3. Avoidance,

4. Accommodation, and

5. Compromise.

When To Use the Conflict Strategies

Competition: When quick and decisive action is necessary.

Collaboration: When your objective is to learn from others.

Avoidance: When an issue is trivial or more important issues are pressing.

Accommodation: When you find that you are wrong, or to show your reasonableness.

Compromise: When goals are important but not worth the effort or potential disruption of more assertive approaches.

Six Steps to Managing Team Conflict

1. *Clarify:* What is the conflict?

2. *Goal:* What is the common goal?

3. *Options:* What are some options?

4. *Remove Barriers:* What are the barriers? What would happen if the barriers were removed?

5. *Agree:* What meets the needs of both parties?

6. *Acknowledge:* What is the solution?

8

MEETING-MANAGEMENT SKILLS

A team meeting is the arena in which the full dynamics of the team are brought to play. It is in this setting that the team communicates, performs, decides, and works out its disagreements. The team's ability to manage its meetings in the most efficient manner is critical to the team's overall success.

Chapter 8 does the following:

- Defines the term "team meeting";
- Describes the purpose of team meetings;
- Discusses methods for planning the meeting;
- Tells how to select the right people to attend;
- Discusses the agenda; and
- Discusses meeting management.

DEFINITION OF A TEAM MEETING

A meeting is an act or process of coming together for a common purpose. A team meeting occurs when team members come together to share information, plan, solve problems, or make decisions.

THE PURPOSE OF THE TEAM MEETING

An effective team meeting begins with a purpose. The manager or team leader must have a good reason for calling a meeting, and then must plan the meeting while keeping the reason for it in mind. Every decision made, from whom to invite to how to run the meeting, revolves around the meeting's purpose. The following are some reasons for conducting a meeting.

- To share information,
- To receive information,
- To generate new ideas,
- To analyze and solve problems,
- To make group decisions,
- To explain problems or goals and gain support,
- To make recommendations, or
- To motivate employees.

PLANNING THE MEETING

Once the purpose of the meeting has been defined, it is important that the manager or team leader determine what outcomes are desired from the meeting. It is useful to plan the meeting with behavioral objectives in mind. For example:

Meeting Purpose: The purpose of this meeting is to understand the new safety system adopted by the team.

Objectives:
1. Team members will understand the purpose of the new safety system.
2. Team members will be familiar with the new equipment used in the new safety system.
3. Team members will understand the three procedures that govern the new safety system.

By using this approach, the manager or team leader can run his or her meeting more efficiently and effectively.

Selecting the Right People To Attend

Other people may be invited to attend team meetings for a number of reasons. Based on the objectives of the meeting, the manager or team leader must consider the following when determining who should attend the meeting.

- Who needs first-hand knowledge of the information the team wants to share?

- From whom does the team need first-hand information?

- Who is affected by the problem to be discussed in the meeting or who else can help to solve the problem?

- Who will be affected by the decision to be made by the team in the meeting?

- Who has the authority to approve the team's decision?

AUTHORS' NOTE

The manager or team leader should consider the number of participants who will attend the meeting. Are there too many or too few participants considering the purpose of the meeting? If the purpose of the meeting is to have the team members hear about a new policy, this can be done in a larger group. However, if the purpose of the meeting is to make a decision about ways of applying a new policy, the manager or team leader should reduce the list of participants to those who are responsible for making the decision.

- Will the person with the authority to approve a decision benefit from the time spent at the meeting?

- Will the person with authority contribute enough to the meeting to justify his or her time?

- Does the person with authority have experience with this type of meeting?

- Does the person with authority have expectations concerning the meeting's outcome?

The Agenda

The agenda—the list of topics to be discussed at the meeting—is essential for effective and efficient team meetings. Without a specific agenda, meetings can become pointless, rambling discussions. Agendas should include the following information:

- The topic(s) to be discussed;
- The person responsible for each topic;
- The time allotted for each topic; and
- The topic category, that is, discussion, information sharing, or decision making.

The agenda should be determined before the meeting by asking the participants for their input. Once the manager or team leader has incorporated the suggested agenda topics, the finalized agenda should be sent to all participants prior to the meeting.

MEETING MANAGEMENT

Once the manager or team leader has determined who will be attending the meeting, and has gathered information about the agenda, the meeting time should be announced. It is important that the announcement be made prior to the meeting so that the participants can reserve time and prepare for the meeting. The announcement should include the following information:

- The meeting's title;

- The names of those who will attend the meeting;
- The manager's or team leader's name and phone number;
- The meeting date;
- The times at which the meeting will begin and end;
- The location of the meeting;
- The meeting's purpose and objectives;
- The preparation required of the participants, if any; and
- What materials the participants should bring, if any.

Time of the Meeting

It is important that the manager or team leader consider the following items when selecting a time for a meeting:

- A time when people will be most energetic (after lunch is a bad time for meetings).
- An appropriate day of the week (usually Monday morning and Friday afternoon are bad).
- Adequate notice (some people hate to go to meetings unprepared).
- The participants' schedules (to avoid scheduling conflicts).

Conducting the Meeting

Effective meetings are the result of good planning. Once the manager or team leader has identified the purpose of the meeting, *who* will attend, *when* the meeting will be held, *where* the meeting will be held, and *how* the meeting should proceed, it is time to have the meeting. The following guidelines are useful for conducting successful meetings.

Room Preparation

The manager or team leader should make sure that the meeting room is ready before the first participant arrives. It is important that the manager or team leader has some lead time in case there are any difficulties in setting up. Other considerations are as follows:

- Make sure that the room is the appropriate size for the meeting.
- Determine whether the chair and table arrangements are adequate and comfortable.
- If audiovisual equipment is to be used, make certain that the right equipment is present and that it works.
- Make certain that all the materials needed are available.
- Post or distribute copies of the meeting's objectives and agenda.

Opening the Meeting

Good meetings always begin on time. The following are some additional suggestions for opening meetings effectively.

- Always start the meeting at the scheduled time. This indicates that you are ready to start doing business.

- Show energy and enthusiasm. It is difficult for the participants to be enthusiastic when the manager or team leader shows low energy.

- Make sure that the participants are introduced to one another. The manager or team leader should spend a few minutes at the beginning of the meeting making introductions, if necessary.

- Reiterate the meeting's objectives and agenda. This is a good time for the manager or team leader to confirm that the participants are aware of them.

- Explain the ground rules that govern the meeting. For example:

— Everyone has a chance to speak.

— Respect the opinions of others.

— Give constructive feedback, not criticism.

— Accept feedback with an open mind.

The manager or team leader should designate who will fill the following roles:

Timekeeper: This person makes sure that time is given to each item on the agenda.

Recorder: This person documents the main points of the meeting on a flip chart so that everyone knows where the time is being spent.

Minute Taker: This person provides a written summary that can be distributed to participants after the meeting.

Closing the Meeting

Closing a meeting is an important step that is often neglected in meeting management. If it is done correctly, it can result in all participants' feeling as if they have accomplished their tasks. The closing provides the manager or team leader with an opportunity to assign action items to participants. It offers a time for team members to review their decision(s).

Like other work, meetings can be evaluated by their productivity and output. Meetings are a critical part of the life of the team. The team's ability to manage meetings effectively will ensure that its time together is well spent.

QUICK REVIEW

Definition of a Team Meeting

A meeting is an act or process of coming together for a common purpose. The following are some reasons for conducting a team meeting.

- To share information,
- To receive information,
- To generate new ideas,
- To analyze and solve problems,
- To reach group decisions,
- To explain problems or goals and gain support,
- To make recommendations, or
- To motivate employees.

Prepare the Agenda

The following items should be considered when preparing the agenda:

- The topic(s) to be discussed;
- The person responsible for each topic;
- The time allotted for each topic; and
- The topic category, that is, discussion, information sharing, or decision making.

Meeting-Site Arrangements

The arrangements given on the following page should be made for the meeting.

- Make sure that the room is the appropriate size for the meeting.
- Determine whether the chair and table arrangements are adequate and comfortable.
- If audiovisual equipment is to be used, make certain that the right equipment is present and that it works.
- Make certain that all the materials needed are available.
- Post or distribute copies of the meeting's objectives and agenda.

9

PROBLEM SOLVING

One of the primary responsibilities of a team is to solve the ongoing problems that impact the team's efforts to achieve its goals. To be effective in solving problems, team members must know what the actual problems are and must have a desire to change or resolve the problems.

Trying to solve a complex problem without a systematic process is like trying to find your way in unknown territory without a map.

Chapter 9 does the following:

- Defines problem solving;
- Presents a seven-step process that can be used by team members in any problem-solving situation; and
- Discusses how to make the process work.

DEFINITION OF PROBLEM SOLVING AND THE PROBLEM-SOLVING PROCESS

Problem solving is the objective examination of issues to arrive at a solution. The problem-solving process is a set of steps by which problems are examined and solved.

THE SEVEN-STEP PROCESS

The first thing a team must do when it is problem solving is to identify the problem it wants to solve. Once the team has identified the problem, it can work toward solving it. The following seven-step process will assist a team in finding a solution.

- Step 1: Define the Problem;

- Step 2: Identify the Desired Future State;
- Step 3: Identify the Forces Acting on the Problem;
- Step 4: Analyze the Forces Acting on the Problem;
- Step 5: Plan a Strategy;
- Step 6: Develop an Action Plan; and
- Step 7: Evaluate.

Step 1: Define the Problem

In the first step, it is important that the team members be able to clearly identify the problem. In addition, it is critical that the team be clear about its desired outcome and the direction of change it wants to pursue. As in any endeavor, working on an ill-defined problem can be a waste of time and resources as well as frustrating.

The team needs to choose a problem that it is strongly committed to solving and over which it has some control. Some questions that the manager or team leader should ask to help define the problem are as follows:

- What is the actual problem (not just the symptoms or results of the problem)?
- Is there more than one problem in the initial problem statement?

It may take some time to identify the real problem, but it is worth the effort. Too often, teams devote time and energy to working on symptoms or results of a problem without adequately identifying the core of the trouble. Effective problem identification is critical if the solution is to work. Also, if the team defines a problem that does not affect the team or that the team has little influence over, the chances of reaching a solution are not good.

If there is more than one actual problem, the manager or team leader will have to take each problem through the problem-solving process. The manager or team leader should then ask the members the following questions:

- What is the impact of the problem on the team?

- What impact does the team have on the problem?

If other teams or individuals are involved, the team will find it helpful to identify all the persons or situations that contribute to the problem. Others may have information that could contribute to the team's understanding of the problem or to the solution. The following are questions that the manager or team leader can ask to find out if others are involved:

- Who else is affected by the problem and in what way?

- Has anyone tried to solve the problem before?

- Why weren't the previous attempts more successful?

- What did work?

These questions are important because they disclose information about the problem's history and the attempts that were made to solve the problem. This kind of information will help the team to avoid past failures and to avoid focusing too much attention on past issues that may no longer exist.

Next, the team will need to define the situation as it is and as the team would like it to be. The following example shows an identified problem statement and a desired outcome statement. Ideally, the outcome statement should be stated in measurable terms.

Problem: Poor member contribution at team meetings.

Problem As It Exists: Only 40 percent of the team is contributing information and ideas during team meetings.

Outcome Statement: 75 percent of the team will contribute ideas and information during team meetings.

Figure 1

At this point, the team will want to reconsider the two statements. If the team is satisfied with its desired outcome statement, it should then answer the next two questions:

- If the change is made, will the problem be solved?
- Is the desired outcome statement manageable and specific enough?

Step 2: Identify the Desired Future State

In the second step, it is important that team members describe the situation as they would like it to be: the desired future state. A precise description of

---

AUTHORS' NOTE

One important consideration the team should be aware of during this step is whether or not it is seeking a solution to the problem or a better way to manage the situation. If the team is clear about its outcome, the forces working on the problem can be better defined.

the desired situation by all team members will serve to identify the goal of the problem-solving effort and the continuum along which change must take place. If the team's statement of the desired future state can be explicitly identified by both quantitative and qualitative information, it will be easier to reach the goal.

Step 3: Identify the Forces Acting on the Problem

In the third step, the team must identify the forces acting on the problem. Forces can be identified by examining individual attitudes, group behaviors, or organizational practices and policies. The greater understanding the team has of the forces working on the problem, the better chance the team will have of finding a solution to it.

At this point, the problem-solving process requires that the forces be categorized as either driving or restraining forces.[1] Driving forces are factors that promote movement in the desired direction; restraining forces are those factors that block the move toward the desired outcome. The following illustration shows both the driving and restraining forces that are working on the problem in Figure 1.

---

[1] Lewin, K. (1969). Quasi-stationary social equilibria and the problem of permanent changes. In W.G. Bennis, K.D. Benne, & R. Chin (Eds.), *The planning of change.* New York: Holt, Rinehart and Winston.

DRIVING AND RESTRAINING FORCES

**Outcome: Increase member participation
to at least 75 percent**

**Problem: Poor member contribution
at team meetings**

DRIVING FORCES	RESTRAINING FORCES
Team members want to do what is right.	Team members want to do what is right but they are not sure what to do.
Team members believe that the more people who contribute, the more ideas for problem solving will be generated.	Team members are not aware of the agenda items for meetings.
Some team members complain about not having time to say anything.	There are some strong people on the team who dominate the conversations.
Team members will not have "ownership" of plans if they do not contribute to developing them.	There is a low level of trust on the team.

Figure 2

Now that the team has considered both the driving and restraining forces, the next step is to analyze the forces in terms of their strengths and weaknesses in moving toward the desired outcome (as stated in Figure 2).

Step 4: Analyze the Forces Acting on the Problem

In the fourth step, the team should review the forces identified and determine if they can be altered in a way that will effectively shift their balance to the desired direction. The team will need to analyze both the driving and restraining forces to determine the ease with which each of these forces can be changed.

There are four team tools that can be used in this step that can facilitate the accurate analysis of the forces. The four team tools are brainstorming, rank ordering, nominal group technique, and multivoting. For a step-by-step application of the above tools, refer to the addendum at the end of this chapter.

Step 5: Plan a Strategy

In the fifth step, the team must work on developing a strategy to change the forces that now exist. There may be slight movement one way or the other, but basically the situation is in a dynamic balance of driving and restraining forces.

To bring about any movement toward the desired outcome, the team must make significant changes in the *restraining* forces. It has been found that decreasing the restraining forces (those opposing change) is much more effective than increasing the driving forces. The greater the team's effort in this direction, the better the team's chances are for achieving the desired change.

In any good strategy, the first thing that the team must consider is the priority of the forces that are under consideration for change. It is a good idea for the team to mark each of the forces with a number, the lowest number representing the highest priority and the highest number representing the least important.

Another consideration is whether or not the force can be changed. If a force cannot be changed in any way, the team should not waste time on it but should move on to the forces that it can impact.

Once the team has examined the forces and decided which one it wants to attack first, there are three issues that must be considered:

- How to increase the driving forces,
- How to decrease the restraining forces, and
- How to change the restraining forces into driving forces.

Increase driving forces. This strategy supports or increases the impact of the driving forces that the team has identified.

Decrease the restraining forces. This strategy targets reducing or changing the factors that present barriers to achieving the desired outcome.

Change the restraining forces into driving forces. This strategy is difficult to implement because it sometimes requires changing attitudes, values, and beliefs. It can be implemented but it requires thoughtful consideration.

Step 6: Develop an Action Plan

In the sixth step, the team must design an action plan that will affect the forces necessary for change. The team's plan should include identifying a team member responsible for the action, a member responsible for the time allocation, and a member ultimately accountable for determining if the action has been accomplished.

Starting with the first force the team chooses to work with, the team needs to consider what has to be done, who will do it, and by when will it be done. If possible, the team should establish more than one action for each force because some action steps will affect the force in different ways.

Actions that are specific have the best chance of being implemented. Generalized attempts are more likely to fail. In addition, the actions that are not assigned to a member to monitor will probably not be implemented.

The last consideration is that the actions the team selects should be seen as achievable. The team members will not complete any actions they believe are not manageable.

Step 7: Evaluate

In the seventh step, the team must evaluate the effectiveness of its plan. The objective of this step is to determine if it will achieve its desired outcome. If the team's action steps do not produce results, they should be reevaluated so that other action steps can be considered.

At the end of this step, the team should know whether the outcome will be achieved. If any adjustments must be made, this is a good time to do it.

SUGGESTED ACTION STEPS TO INCREASE MEMBERS' CONTRIBUTIONS AT TEAM MEETINGS

Force for Which Action Step Is Planned	Action Steps	Person Responsible for Action Step	Time Table
Team members want to do what is right.	Team members and team leader discuss different behaviors for doing the right thing.	All team	Next meeting
Team members believe that the more people contribute, the more ideas for problem solving will be generated.	Team members and team leader discuss the importance of every member's contribution.	All team	Next meeting
Some team members complain about not having the time to say anything.	Team members and team leader discuss the task and relationship behaviors in team dynamics.	All team	Next scheduled team-building session
Team members will not buy in if they do not contribute to developing plans.	Team members and team leader discuss effective communication and feedback strategies for the team.	All team	Next meeting

MAKING THE PROCESS WORK

The problem-solving process discussed in this chapter is only as good as the team that attempts to use it. An effective problem-solving team must comprise individuals who feel free to express their ideas and opinions in an atmosphere of openness and sharing. Paying attention to the dynamics of the team is an important task for the manager or team leader when team members are working together. Discussing who, what, and how the team operates helps to facilitate open communication, trust, and commitment to the team and the problem-solving process.

QUICK REVIEW

Definition of Problem Solving and the Problem-Solving Process

Problem solving is the objective examination of issues to arrive at a solution. The problem-solving process is a set of steps by which problems are examined and solved.

The Seven-Step Process

- Step 1: Define the Problem;
- Step 2: Identify the Desired Future State;
- Step 3: Identify the Forces Acting on the Problem;
- Step 4: Analyze the Forces Acting on the Problem;
- Step 5: Plan a Strategy;
- Step 6: Develop an Action Plan; and
- Step 7: Evaluate.

Making the Process Work

An effective problem-solving team must comprise individuals who feel free to express their ideas and opinions in an atmosphere of openness and sharing.

ADDENDUM

PROBLEM SOLVING

TEAM TOOLS

There are four team tools that can be used to facilitate the accurate analysis of the forces. The four team tools are as follows:

- Brainstorming,
- Rank ordering,
- Nominal group technique, and
- Multivoting

Brainstorming: To generate, clarify, and evaluate a sizable list of ideas, opinions, issues, or various other concerns.

Rank ordering: To assign projects to team members and to assign priorities for group decision-making by developing a visual display of individual and team rankings of ideas.

Nominal group technique: To reach consensus within a structured situation.

Multivoting: To assign projects to team members in order of priority and with a high degree of group agreement.

Brainstorming

Definition: A group technique to generate creative ideas in an interactive process.

Purpose: Generate options to be considered when making decisions.

Guidelines

- Make sure that all team members understand the objective of the brainstorming session.
- Encourage active participation of all members.
- Develop a high energy, enthusiastic climate.
- Avoid discussing, criticizing, or complimenting ideas as they are presented.
- Encourage creative thinking, including eccentric ideas.
- Build and expand on the ideas of others.
- Record all ideas on a flip chart exactly as they are presented.
- Do not end the session if the members cannot think of ideas immediately. Generate as long a list of ideas as possible.

How To Conduct a Brainstorming Session

1. Review the following steps for brainstorming.
2. Clarify the objective of the team's brainstorming session.
3. Have team members take turns calling out ideas.
4. Record each idea on a flip chart exactly as it is presented.
5. Members do not need to contribute an idea if they cannot think of one quickly.
6. After all ideas have been presented, the team clarifies the list by discussing the ideas to ensure that all members have the same understanding of each idea. Eliminate duplications.

Rank Ordering

Definition: A group decision-making technique that provides a visual display of the members' and the team's rankings of ideas in a short list.

Purpose: To prioritize a list of ideas.

Guidelines

- Team members decide on the criteria for ranking ideas.

- Team members must rank all the ideas on the list.

When recorded on a flip chart, the members' rankings visually display the extent of agreement among members on the ranking of ideas. If rank ordering reveals considerable disagreement among members, a second ranking may be carried out after a discussion and debate of the ideas.

How To Conduct Rank Ordering

1. Review the following steps for rank ordering.
2. Team members must agree on the criteria for ranking ideas.
3. Identify each idea on the list with a letter of the alphabet.
4. Team members individually list the letters on a piece of paper and indicate the rank of each idea next to the letter, with "1" being the first choice, "2" the second choice, and so on.
5. Each team member takes a turn calling out the number that indicates his or her ranking of each

idea. The rankings are recorded and added on the flip chart.

6. The team analyzes the rankings, looking at the total for each idea as well as individual votes.

Nominal Group Technique

Definition: A structured, group decision-making process used to assign priorities by ranking a group of items.

Purpose: To generate options to be considered in making decisions.

Guidelines

- Identify in advance the questions to be addressed.
- Plan to address only one topic per meeting.
- Allow no comments or discussions during the recording of ideas.
- Focus on clarification of meaning, not on arguing points, during the group discussion.
- Limit the members' discussion to brief explanations of logic or analysis of an item and brief statements for agreeing or disagreeing with the item.

How To Conduct the Nominal Group Technique

1. Review the following steps for group technique.
2. Have each team member write his or her ideas on a piece of paper.
3. Record the members' ideas on a flip chart. Do not allow the group to discuss the ideas.

4. Conduct a group discussion to clarify ideas. Do not allow members to argue for their ideas.

5. Vote to establish the priority or rank of each item.

6. Discuss the vote and eliminate lower ranked items.

7. Continue rounds of voting and discussion, eliminating less supported items until a consensus decision is reached.

Multivoting

Definition: A group decision-making technique designed to reduce a long list of ideas to a manageable number of ideas.

Purpose: To reduce a long list of ideas.

Guidelines

- Team members decide on the criteria for selecting ideas.

- Each member votes for an agreed number of ideas. The team decides how many ideas each member will vote for. A common rule used is that each member will vote for 25 percent of the total number of ideas.

- Team members can give only one vote to an individual idea and should use all the votes agreed on by the team.

- The ideas with the most votes receive further consideration.

- If a relatively long list of ideas remains, a second vote may be taken after a discussion and debate of the ideas.

How To Conduct Multivoting

1. Review the following steps for multivoting.
2. Team members must agree on the criteria for selecting ideas.
3. Identify each idea on the list with a letter of the alphabet.
4. Team members agree on the number of ideas that each member can vote for.
5. Each member lists his or her vote on a piece of paper, listing the letter of each item selected. Each member takes a turn calling out the letter of the items for which he or she voted.
6. Votes are recorded with a tally mark next to the item on the flip chart.
7. The team decides which ideas should receive further consideration.

10

THE POLITICS OF PARTICIPATION

Because change is often resisted by many individuals within organizations, an understanding of the politics involved in changing an organization's culture is necessary if teams are to succeed. We call this process the "politics of participation."

Chapter 10 does the following:

- Defines the "politics of participation";
- Examines eleven critical factors that are essential when considering a team-structured organization; and
- Describes four critical roles that individuals can play in the change process.

DEFINITION OF THE POLITICS OF PARTICIPATION

The politics of participation refers to the competing interests involved when teams play a role in deciding organizational undertakings. Because politics is defined as competition between interest groups or individuals for power and leadership, the addition of team participation in the decision process changes the nature of the organizational politics.

ELEVEN CRITICAL FACTORS

Organizations vary greatly in their levels of readiness to support a team culture. However, the following eleven factors are critical in predicting the organization's readiness to use teams. The greater the number of "yes" responses to the factors described on the following page, the greater the probability of success in establishing a team culture.

1. *Management's Philosophy and Core Values.* Do the mission statement and guiding principles of the organization foster the concept of work teams and group participation at all levels within the organization?

_____Yes   _____No

2. *Organizational Structure.* Does the organization have a relatively flat structure with few levels of management?

_____Yes   _____No

3. *Problem-Solving Groups.* Do task forces, quality circles, or other groups that utilize employee participation exist within the organization?

_____Yes   _____No

4. *Information Systems.* Does the method for information sharing and exchange provide all employees with the means to coordinate and manage their work efficiently?

_____Yes   _____No

5. *Physical and Technical Design.* Is the work environment safe, pleasant, and centralized?

_____Yes   _____No

6. *Reward Systems.* Does the organization offer pay incentives for increased job knowledge, skill development, or productivity gains?

_____Yes   _____No

7. *Personnel Policies.* Are issues related to work hours, flextime, benefits, layoffs, discipline, and other personnel issues handled by management in a way that is satisfactory to employees?

_____Yes   _____No

8. *Career Systems.* Does the organization offer counseling services to employees concerning career development or training?

_____Yes   _____No

9. *Employee-Selection Systems.* Does the organization have adequate hiring practices, policies, and procedures established for recruiting, selecting, and retaining a motivated work force?

_____Yes   _____No

10. *Training Orientation.* Is the organization committed to training and developing its employees?

_____Yes   _____No

11. *Leadership Style.* Does the organization utilize a participatory leadership style?

_____Yes   _____No

It is important to understand that this overview of critical factors does not reflect the organization's overall effectiveness or productivity, but it will predict the organization's readiness to develop and sustain a team culture.

CRITICAL ROLES IN THE CHANGE PROCESS

When change occurs within an organization, there are four roles individuals can play that are critical to the change process. The roles are as follows:

- The sponsor,
- The change agent,
- The target, and
- The champion.

The Sponsor

The sponsor is defined as the individual or group that uses organizational power and influence to legitimize the change. Sponsors are critical to a successful effort at the beginning of a change project. Without their power and influence, the likelihood of change is low. Within an organization, the chief executive officer (CEO), vice president, plant manager, or director often assume the role of sponsor. Because of their power and influence, sponsors are notorious for initiating major organizational disruptions by issuing decrees to the targets and bypassing the implementation-planning process and the role of the change agent.

The Change Agent

The change agent is defined as the person or group that is responsible for implementing or helping to implement the change. Change agents generally demonstrate their greatest contributions when they act as planners, diagnosticians, implementors, translators, trouble-shooters, negotiators, and buffer zones for sponsors and targets. Directors, middle managers, supervisors, team leaders, and human-resource professionals often hold the change-agent role in a major change effort.

AUTHORS' NOTE

Two mistakes most frequently made by change agents are (1) to change something about the decision or the implementation of the decision without gaining a sponsor's understanding or approval, and (2) attempting to change more or less than the sponsor actually understood or approved.

The Change Target

The change target is defined as the individual or group that, as a result of the change, will have to alter major elements of how they do their work. The change targets are often middle managers, first-line supervisors, team leaders, and workers. Change targets are most important when the change is implemented. At this point, they control whether or not the intended modifications will actually occur.

Many organizations, unfortunately, initiate significant shifts in operations without a clear definition of who the target population is, what its frame of reference is, how it will be affected, and to what degree it is ready to accept or resist the change. Every minute of time spent assessing, involving, and planning for the change will increase the likelihood of a successful implementation.

The Champion

The champion is defined as the person who wants to achieve a change but lacks sufficient sponsorship or organizational power. A change that a champion wants cannot and does not occur until the champion secures a sponsor. Advocacy without sponsorship can be described as:

- Hope without power,
- Willingness without ability,
- Solutions without a problem,
- Answers without a question, or
- Desire without resources.

Any of the three previous roles can serve as champion. Sponsors can be their own champions by becoming aware of the necessity to change through observing critical events, reading relevant reports, anticipating shifting market demands, and watching other organizations. Sometimes the advocating influence comes from an employee or a group of employees, from peers of a sponsor in another part of the organization, or from others higher in the organizational structure.

A champion brings the idea of change to the attention of the organization. If the idea receives sufficient sponsorship it becomes a legitimate change that is implemented. Champions do not generate changes; only sponsors have that power. In general, advocacy can go up through an organization; however, significant change occurs only from the top down.

QUICK REVIEW

Definition of the Politics of Participation

The politics of participation refers to the competing interests involved when teams play a role in deciding organizational undertakings.

Eleven Critical Factors

Organizations vary greatly in their levels of readiness to support a team culture. The following eleven factors are critical in predicting whether or not an organization is ready to support a team culture.

1. Management's philosophy and core values,

2. Organizational structure,

3. Problem-solving groups,

4. Information systems,

5. Physical and technical design,

6. Reward systems,

7. Personnel policies,

8. Career systems,

9. Employee-selection systems,

10. Training orientation, and

11. Leadership style.

Critical Roles in the Change Process

When change occurs in organizations, there are four roles individuals can play. They are as follows:

- The sponsor,
- The change agent,
- The target, and
- The champion.

Conclusion

This book is designed to give managers, supervisors, and team leaders the conceptual and practical knowledge they need to manage an effective team-development effort.

Although most organizations could benefit from using teams, we recognize that some individuals, groups, and organizations are not ready to implement teams or are not able to use teams effectively.

It is clear that team-development efforts should not be initiated if the organizational climate is highly resistant to a new way of doing business, such as the team approach.

Today, we still find many companies reluctant to endorse the team concept, although organizational research supports the use of teams. We believe that those businesses that fail to change today will not be in business tomorrow.

Editor: Socorro P. Gonzalez

Production Editor: Dawn Kilgore

Cover Design, Interior Design, and Illustrations:
Lee Ann Hubbard

Page Composition: Lee Ann Hubbard

This book was edited and formatted using 486 platforms with 8MB RAM and high-resolution, dual-page monitors. The copy was produced using WordPerfect software; pages composed with Ventura software. The text is set in twelve on fourteen and one-half Caxton and the headings are Futura Condensed Bold. Camera-ready copy was output on a 1200-dpi laser imagesetter by Pfeiffer and Company.